James Andrew Murray

A Treatise on Proceedings in the United States Courts

James Andrew Murray

A Treatise on Proceedings in the United States Courts

ISBN/EAN: 9783337380212

Printed in Europe, USA, Canada, Australia, Japan

Cover: Foto ©Suzi / pixelio.de

More available books at **www.hansebooks.com**

A TREATISE

ON

Proceedings in the United States Courts,

DESIGNED FOR THE USE OF

ATTORNEYS AND COUNSELORS PRACTICING THEREIN,

AND ALSO FOR THE

DEPUTIES OF THE UNITED STATES MARSHALS,

AND OTHER OFFICERS OF THE UNITED STATES,

WITH

PRACTICAL FORMS AND AN APPENDIX.

By JAMES ANDREW MURRAY.

ALBANY:
WEED, PARSONS AND COMPANY,
PUBLISHERS AND PRINTERS,
1869.

Entered according to Act of Congress, in the year eighteen hundred and sixty-nine, by
JAMES ANDREW MURRAY
In the Clerk's Office of the District Court of the United States for the Northern District of New York.

TO THE

MEMORY OF MY BROTHER,

JOHN B. MURRAY,

THIS WORK IS

AFFECTIONATELY DEDICATED.

PREFACE.

A work of practical utility, as this is intended to be, requires but few words by way of preface or explanation of its plan or design.

For convenience of reference, I have divided the work into four parts. In Part I will be found — under their appropriate heads — matters of general information pertaining to the office of Deputy Marshal. In Parts II, III and IV, are set forth the various forms for returns to process now in use in the Northern District of New York, to wit: In Part II, forms in *Information* suits — that is, where property is seized *on land;* in Part III, forms in *Admiralty* cases — or, where property is seized *on water;* and in Part IV, miscellaneous forms in civil and criminal cases.

The Author has been induced to commence this work from a belief in its usefulness and necessity. And, although he is aware that the practice in the different districts of the United States is not similar to that in this District, he is confident that the greater part of this book will be found of practical use in all. It was at first intended to make it a book of forms;. but afterwards it was deemed expedient to publish it in the form it is now presented.

With the hope that this work may meet with a kind reception, it is submitted to the favorable consideration of those for whom it is designed.

J. A. M.

BUFFALO, *October*, 1869.

A LIST OF THE ABBREVIATIONS USED.

Abb. Adm	Abbott's Admiralty Reports.
Blatch. C. C.	Blatchford's Circuit Court Reports.
Brock. Marsh	Brockenbrough's Marshals' Decisions.
Burn. (Wis.)	Burnett's Wisconsin Reports.
Cliff	Clifford's Circuit Court Reports.
Cranch C. Ct	Cranch's Circuit Court Reports.
Cranch	Cranch's Supreme Court Reports.
Gall	Gallison's Circuit Court Reports.
Hempst	Hempstead's Circuit Court Reports.
How	Howard's Supreme Court Reports.
Id	Idem — the same.
Ibid	Ibidem — in the same case.
Op. Atty. Gen	Opinions of Attorneys-General.
Pet. C. C	Peters' Circuit Court Reports.
Pet	Peters' Supreme Court Reports.
McL	McLean's Circuit Court Reports.
Sprague	Sprague's Decisions.
Stat. at L	U. S. Statutes at Large.
U. S. Const	Constitution of the United States.
Wall. C. Ct	Wallace's Circuit Court Reports.
Wall	Wallace's Supreme Court Reports.
Wheat	Wheaton's Supreme Court Reports.

JUSTICES OF THE SUPREME COURT.

Chief-Justice.
Hon. SALMON P. CHASE, Washington, D. C.

Associates.
Hon. SAMUEL NELSON, Cooperstown, N. Y.
Hon. ROBERT C. GRIER, Philadelphia, Pa.
Hon. NATHAN CLIFFORD, Portland, Me.
Hon. NOAH H. SWAYNE, Columbus, O.
Hon. SAMUEL F. MILLER, Keokuk, Iowa.
Hon. DAVID DAVIS, Bloomington, Ill.
Hon. STEPHEN J. FIELD, San Francisco, Cal.

Clerk of the Court.
D. W. MIDDLETON, Washington, D. C.

United States Attorney-General.
Hon. E. R. HOAR, Washington, D. C.

UNITED STATES DISTRICT JUDGES.

Alabama — NORTHERN, SOUTHERN AND MIDDLE DISTRICTS.
Hon. RICHARD BUSTEED, MOBILE.

Arkansas — EASTERN AND WESTERN DISTRICTS.
Hon. HENRY C. CALDWELL, LITTLE ROCK.

California.
Hon. OGDEN HOFFMAN, SAN FRANCISCO.

Connecticut.
Hon. WM. D. SHIPMAN, HARTFORD.

Delaware.
Hon. WILLARD HALL, WILMINGTON.

Florida — NORTHERN DISTRICT.
Hon. PHILIP FRASER, JACKSONVILLE.

SOUTHERN DISTRICT.
Hon. THOS. J. BOYNTON, KEY WEST.

Georgia — NORTHERN AND SOUTHERN DISTRICTS.
Hon. JOHN ERSKINE, SAVANNAH.

Illinois — NORTHERN DISTRICT.
Hon. THOS. DRUMMOND, CHICAGO.

SOUTHERN DISTRICT.
Hon. SAMUEL H. TREAT, SPRINGFIELD.

DISTRICT JUDGES.

Indiana.
HON. WALTER Q. GRESHAM, NEW ALBANY.

Iowa.
HON. JAMES M. LOVE, OTTUMWA.

Kansas.
HON. MARK W. DELAHAY, TOPEKA.

Kentucky.
HON. BLAND BALLARD, LOUISVILLE.

Louisiana.
HON. E. H. DURELL, NEW ORLEANS.

Maine.
HON. EDMUND FOX, PORTLAND.

Maryland.
HON. WM. FELL GILES, BALTIMORE.

Massachusetts.
HON. JOHN LOWELL, NEWTON.

Michigan — EASTERN DISTRICT.
HON. ROSS WILKINS, DETROIT.

WESTERN DISTRICT.
HON. S. L. WITHEY, GRAND RAPIDS.

Minnesota.
HON. R. R. NELSON, ST. PAUL.

Mississippi — NORTHERN AND SOUTHERN DISTRICTS.
HON. ROBERT A. HILL, OXFORD.

Missouri — EASTERN DISTRICT.
HON. SAMUEL TREAT, ST. LOUIS.

DISTRICT JUDGES.

WESTERN DISTRICT.
HON. ARNOLD KREKEL, JEFFERSON CITY.

Nebraska.
HON. ELMER S. DUNDY, FALLS CITY.

Nevada.
HON. A. W. BALDWIN, VIRGINIA.

New Hampshire.
HON. DANIEL CLARK, MANCHESTER.

New Jersey.
HON. RICHARD S. FIELD, PRINCETON.

New York — NORTHERN DISTRICT.
HON. NATHAN K. HALL, BUFFALO.

SOUTHERN DISTRICT.
HON. SAMUEL BLATCHFORD, NEW YORK.

EASTERN DISTRICT.
HON. CHAS. L. BENEDICT, BROOKLYN.

North Carolina.
HON. GEORGE W. BROOKS, ELIZABETH CITY.

Ohio — NORTHERN DISTRICT.
HON. CHARLES T. SHERMAN, CLEVELAND.

SOUTHERN DISTRICT.
HON. HUMPHREY H. LEAVITT, CINCINNATI.

Oregon.
HON. MATTHEW P. DEADY, PORTLAND.

Pennsylvania — EASTERN DISTRICT.
HON. JOHN CADWALADER, PHILADELPHIA.

DISTRICT JUDGES.

Western District.
Hon. WILSON McCANDLESS, Pittsburgh.

Rhode Island.
Hon. JOHN P. KNOWLES.

South Carolina.
Hon. GEORGE S. BRYAN, Charleston.

Tennessee — Eastern, Western and Middle Districts.
Hon. CONNALLY F. TRIGG, Memphis.

Texas — Eastern District.
Hon. JOHN C. WATROUS, Galveston.

Western District.
Hon. THOMAS H. DUVAL, Austin.

Vermont.
Hon. DAVID A. SMALLEY, Burlington.

Virginia.
Hon. JOHN C. UNDERWOOD, Richmond.

West Virginia.
Hon. JOHN G. JACKSON, Parkersburg.

Wisconsin.
Hon. ANDREW G. MILLER, Milwaukee.

TABLE OF CONTENTS.

	PAGE.
Preface	5
List of Abbreviations	7
List of the Justices of the U. S. Supreme Court	9
List of the Judges of the U. S. District Courts	11
Table of Contents	15

PART I.

	PAGE
General information	17
SECTION 1. Of admiralty	22
2. Of affidavits and depositions	24
3. Of arrest	28
4. Of attachment	31
5. Of bail	33
6. Of distress warrants	38
7. Of execution	43
8. Of extradition	49
9. Of fees,	52
10. Of indictment,	53
11. Of interest	54
12. Of imprisonment for debt	55
13. Of jails	56
14. Of judgments	58
15. Of juries	59
16. Of limitation	64
17. Of name	68
18. Of oaths	68
19. Of pardon	69
20. Of powers, duties and liabilities of Marshals	71

TABLE OF CONTENTS.

	PAGE.
SECTION 21. Of prisoners	77
22. Of process	79
23. Of seizure cases	81
24. Of subpœnas and witnesses	83

PART II.

Forms for returns in information suits 91

PART III.

Forms for returns in admiralty cases 103

PART IV.

Miscellaneous forms, and forms in civil and criminal cases 121

Appendix (A) 149
Appendix (B) 165
Index 171

A TREATISE

ON

PROCEEDINGS IN THE UNITED STATES COURTS,

DESIGNED FOR THE USE OF

ATTORNEYS AND COUNSELORS PRACTICING THEREIN, AND ALSO
FOR THE DEPUTIES OF THE UNITED STATES MARSHALS,
AND OTHER OFFICERS OF THE UNITED STATES.
WITH PRACTICAL FORMS AND AN
APPENDIX.

PART I.

GENERAL INFORMATION.

On receiving his appointment, and before entering on the duties of his office, the Deputy Marshal is required to take the following oath or affirmation, viz.:

"I,   , do solemnly swear [or affirm] that I will faithfully execute all lawful precepts directed to the Marshal of the District of   under the authority of the United States, and true returns make, and in all things well and truly, and without malice or partiality, perform the duties of the office of Marshal's Deputy of the District of   , during my continuance in said office, and take only my lawful fees. So help me God.

"And I do further solemnly swear [or affirm] that I will support the Constitution of the United States. So help me God." (Act Sept. 24, 1789; 1 Stat. at L. 87, § 27; Act June 1, 1789: 1 Stat. at L. 23, § 1.)

This oath should be taken before the District Judge; but when a Deputy Marshal shall "reside and be" more than twenty miles from the place where the District Judge of his District shall "reside and be," the oath may be administered and taken by and before any judge or justice of any State court within the same District, or before any justice of the peace having authority therein, and, being certified by him to the said District Judge, shall be as effectual as if administered or taken before the District Judge. (Act. Feb. 28, 1799; 1 Stat. at L. 625, § 2.)

It may also be taken before any United States Commissioner.

By Act of Congress, approved July 2, 1862 (12 Stat. at L. 502, § 1), the Deputy Marshal is also required, before entering upon the duties of his office, to take and subscribe the following oath or affirmation, viz.:

"I,   , do solemnly swear [or affirm] that I have never voluntarily borne arms against the United States since I have been a citizen thereof; that I have voluntarily given no aid, countenance, counsel or encouragement to persons engaged in armed hostility thereto; that I have neither sought nor accepted, nor attempted to exercise the functions of, any office whatever, under any authority or pretended authority in hostility to the United States; that I have not yielded a voluntary support to any pretended government, authority, power or constitution within the United States, hostile or inimical thereto.

And I do further swear [or affirm] that, to the best of my knowledge and ability, I will support and defend the Constitution of the United States against all enemies, foreign and domestic; that I will bear true faith and allegiance to the same; that I take this obligation freely, without any mental reservation or purpose of evasion, and that I will well and faithfully discharge the duties of the office on which I am about to enter. So help me God."

The Deputy is also obliged to execute a bond to the Marshal for the faithful performance of his duties, — the penal sum whereof is whatever the Marshal of the District may require, but is usually from five to ten thousand dollars. (See form No. 27.)

Every Deputy should provide himself with two dockets, in one of which should be entered all *criminal cases*, showing what has been done in each, the disposition made thereof and the fees therein; and in the other should likewise be entered all *civil cases*. It will also be found convenient to have a scrap book, in which should be placed copies of all legal notices published by the Deputy.

It is of very great importance that all papers should be returned in as clean a state as when placed in the hands of the Deputy, and that his returns should be indorsed on some part of the process, other than that whereon is the indorsement of the court. He should also indorse on all process placed in his hands, the hour of the day, day of the month, and the year, of its receipt by him, and *promptly execute and return* the same to the Marshal. Where proof of publication of any notice is required, the same should be obtained and annexed to the process at the time of making return thereof.

It very often happens that process of arrest and execution are given to the Deputy in the first instance, instead of being sent to the Marshal. In such case, the Deputy should, as soon as possible, inform the

Marshal of the fact, giving the title of the case, nature of the writ, the amount sued for or to be collected, the name of the attorney, and such other information as will be requisite for the Marshal to know and enable him to make the proper entries on his books.

In Commissioners' Courts, United States witnesses should be paid as soon as they are discharged by the Commissioner. The Deputy takes a receipt on *duplicate* pay-rolls for the amount paid each witness. If more than four witnesses have been paid, the District Attorney's certificate should be obtained as to their necessity and materiality. (See page 84.) The pay-rolls should then be forwarded to the Marshal as vouchers for such payments.

As soon as a case is determined before a Commissioner, the Deputy should forward to the Marshal the warrants and subpœnas served by him, with the proper returns thereon indorsed, and give the result of the examination, whether the prisoner was discharged, gave bail, or was committed to jail, always stating *for what term* the recognizance was taken, or the committal made. This is necessary to enable the Marshal to make correct estimates for term expenses, and also to know to whom to send subsequent process in the case. He should also see that the Commissioner's minutes, with a correct list of the names and residence of the witnesses who will be required before the Grand Jury, are forwarded to the District Attorney, without delay.

It is proper to state here, that, in accordance with the provisions of the law requiring witnesses to be subpœnaed to testify generally on the part of the

GENERAL INFORMATION. 21

United States, the name of a witness is inserted in a subpœna *but once for the same term;* unless he is required to be summoned *duces tecum,* after having been theretofore subpœnaed, and unless, also, he has been discharged, and it is afterwards ascertained that he will be needed in another cause. (See page 86.)

When subpœnas are needed on the part of the United States, the District Attorney issues a *præcipe* to the Clerk of the court wherein the suit is pending, and the Clerk makes out the subpœnas accordingly.

Under no circumstances should the Deputy alter process, or allow the same to be altered, after it comes into his hands. No name should be inserted in a subpœna unless it is done by the Clerk. If additional witnesses are needed, the Deputy should inform the District Attorney; but should not subpœna them without process.

When a Deputy Marshal is present at a term of the court, and has cases for trial, or for the Grand Jury, he should be constant in his attendance, in order that the District Attorney can have his aid in keeping the witnesses at his command, and can consult with him when necessary.

SECTION I.

ADMIRALTY.

In any case brought in the courts of the United States, exercising jurisdiction in admiralty, where a warrant of arrest, or other process *in rem*, shall be issued, it shall be the duty of the Marshal to stay the execution of such process, or to discharge the property arrested, if the same has been levied, on receiving from the claimant of the same a bond or stipulation, in double the amount claimed by the libellant, with sufficient surety, to be approved by the Judge of the said court, or, in his absence, by the Collector of the port, conditioned to abide and answer the decree of the court in such cause; and such bond or stipulation shall be returned to the said court, and judgment on the same, both against the principal and sureties, may be recovered at the time of rendering the decree in the original cause, etc. (Act March 3, 1847; 9 Stat. at L. 181.)

This does not, however, apply to suits for forfeiture, but only to private suits *in rem*.

If a bond is not given as above stated, the Marshal is required to publish the notice mentioned in form No. 14.

No delivery on bail can legally be made, where the United States is a party, without due notice to the District Attorney. (*Ex parte Robbins*, 2 Gall. 320.)

When the Marshal holds a vessel, by virtue of two warrants to arrest, in different suits, the custody fees are to be charged equally upon the two suits. (*The John Walls, Jr.*, Sprague, 178.)

Where a vessel, seized under a warrant from the District Court, continued in the custody of the Marshal until the case was disposed of in the Circuit Court, the Marshal had no right to effect insurance on the vessel, while so remaining in his custody, at the expense of either party, without their consent.

Money paid by the Marshal for such insurance cannot be allowed in the taxable costs. (*Burke* v. *Brig M. P. Rich*, 1 Cliff. 509.)

Under rules 47 and 48 of the United States District Court for the Southern District of New York, notice of sale under a *venditioni exponas* (except on condemnation of property on seizure by the United States) must be published for *six* days; and the sale will be set aside if this full number of publications is not made. (*The Hornet*, 1 Abb. Adm. 57.)

It is not a sufficient return to a *venditioni exponas*, " that A B. to whom the property was struck off at the sale, has neglected and refused to comply with the terms of sale." (*Wortman* v. *Conyngham*, Pet. C. C. 241.)

It is the duty of the Marshal to offer the property at sale again, if he had time to do so; and if not, by a proper return, enable the plaintiff to take out an *alias* (Ibid.)

SECTION II.

AFFIDAVITS AND DEPOSITIONS.

All of the courts of the United States shall have power to impose and administer necessary oaths and affirmations. (Act Sept. 24, 1789, 1 Stat. at L. 83, § 17.)

The Commissioners appointed by the Circuit Courts are authorized "to take acknowledgments of bail and affidavits" (act Feb. 20, 1812, 2 Stat. at L. 679, § 1); "to take affidavits and bail in civil causes, to be used in the several District Courts of the United States" (act March 1, 1817, 3 Stat. at L. 350, § 1); and also in civil causes, to take depositions of persons *de bene esse.* (Id.)

By act of February 26, 1853 (10 Stat. at L. 163, § 1), the Clerks of the District and Circuit Courts respectively, *ex officio*, are "authorized and empowered to administer oaths, take acknowledgments, take and certify affidavits and depositions in the same manner as Commissioners."

Notaries Public are also authorized to "take depositions, and do such other acts in relation to evidence to be used in the courts of the United States, in the same manner, and with the same effect, as Commissioners to take acknowledgments of bail and affidavits may now lawfully take or do." (Act July 29, 1854, 10 Stat. at L. 315, § 1.)

Under the last mentioned provision of the law, affidavits taken before Notaries Public *having a seal* are accepted by the United States Courts in the Northern District of New York.

Registers in bankruptcy shall have power to administer oaths in all cases and in relation to all matters in which oaths may be administered by Commissioners of the Circuit Courts of the United States, and such Commissioners may take proof of debts in bankruptcy in all cases, subject to the revision of such proofs by the Register and by the court, according to the provisions of the bankruptcy act. (Act July 27, 1868, 2 Pamphlet Laws, 228, § 3.) See "Oaths."

The Clerks of the District and Circuit Courts, in the absence or in case of the disability of the Judges, are authorized to take "the affidavits of all surveyors relative to their reports, and to administer oaths to all persons identifying papers found on board of vessels or elsewhere, to be used on trial in admiralty causes." (Act May 3, 1792, 1 Stat. at L. 278, § 10.)

In case of the District Judge in any District being unable to discharge his duties, * * the District Clerk of such District shall be authorized and empowered, by leave or order of the Circuit Judge of the Circuit in which such District is included, to take, during such disability of the District Judge, all examinations and depositions of witnesses, and make all necessary rules and orders preparatory to the final hearing of all causes of admiralty and maritime jurisdiction. (Act March 2, 1809, 2 Stat. at L. 535, § 3.)

When the testimony of any person shall be necessary in any civil cause depending in any District, in any court of the United States, who shall live at a greater distance from the place of trial than one hundred miles, or is bound on a voyage to sea, or is about to go out of the United States, or out of such District, and to a greater distance from the place of trial than as aforesaid, before the time of trial, or is ancient or very infirm, the deposition of such person may be taken *de bene esse*, before *any Justice or Judge of any of the courts of the United States, or before any Chancellor, Justice or Judge of a Supreme or Superior Court, Mayor or chief magistrate of a city, or Judge of a County Court or Court of Common Pleas of any of the United States*, not being of counsel or attorney to either of the parties, or interested in the event of the cause. (Act Sept. 24, 1789, 1 Stat. at L. 88, § 30.)

Every Secretary of Legation and consular officer is hereby authorized, whenever he shall be required or may deem it necessary or proper so to do, at the post, port, place, or within the limits of his legation, consulate or commercial agency, to administer to or take from any person an oath, affirmation, affidavit or deposition, and also to perform any notarial act or acts such as any notary public is required or authorized by law to do or perform within the United States; and every such oath, affirmation, affidavit, deposition and notarial act administered, sworn, affirmed, taken, had or done, by or before any such officer, when certified under his hand and seal of office, shall be as good, valid, effectual, and of like force and effect within the United States, to all intents and purposes, as if such oath, affirmation, affidavit, deposition or notarial act had been administered, sworn, affirmed, taken, had or done, by or before any other person within the United States duly authorized and competent thereto; and if any person shall willfully and corruptly commit perjury, or by any means procure any person to commit perjury in any such oath, affirmation, affidavit or deposition, within the intent and meaning of any act of Congress now or hereafter made, such offender may be charged, proceeded against, tried, convicted, and dealt with in any District of the United States, in the same manner, in all respects, as if such offense had been committed in the United States, before any officer duly authorized therein to administer or take such oath, affirmation, affidavit or deposition, and shall be subject to the same punishment and disability therefor as are or shall be prescribed by any such act for such offense; and any document purporting to have affixed, impressed or subscribed thereto or thereon, the seal and signature of the officer administering or taking the same in testimony thereof, shall be admitted in evidence without proof of any such seal or signature being genuine or of the official character of such person; and if any person shall forge any such seal or signature, or shall tender in evidence any such document with a false or counterfeit seal or signature thereto, knowing the same to be false or counterfeit, he shall be deemed and taken to be guilty of a misdemeanor, and, on conviction, shall be imprisoned not exceeding three years and not less than one year, and fined in a sum not to exceed three thousand dollars, and may be charged, proceeded against, tried, convicted and dealt with therefor, in the District where he may be arrested or in custody. (Act Aug. 18, 1856, 11 Stat. at L. 61, § 24.)

SECTION III.

ARREST.

Of this it is not necessary to treat at length, as every Deputy Marshal is presumed to be familiar with the mode of arrest and commitment.

But there are several matters which require particular attention on the part of the Deputy, viz. :

First. In making an arrest on a *bailable capias*, the Deputy should take a bond to the Marshal for the amount named in the writ, and conditioned that the defendant shall put in special bail within twenty days after the return day thereof and perfect such bail if required. (See form No. 34.) If the defendant *cannot* give bail, he should be committed to the *common jail of the county wherein the arrest was made*, and the proper return indorsed on the *capias*. (See form No. 32.) If he *does* give bail, he is not required to appear at court on the return day of the *capias*. He has merely to enter his appearance with the Clerk, and serve notice thereof on the District Attorney (which can be done by his attorney), and put in special bail within twenty days after the return day. A party cannot be arrested on a *non-bailable capias*. The Deputy merely makes service by showing the original writ to the defendant and leaving with him a copy thereof. The forms of both writs are the same, and the only apparent difference is in the one being indorsed *bailable capias* and the other *non-bailable capias*. They may, however, be distinguished by the cause of action mentioned in the writ, — for instance, a suit to recover a penalty is *bailable*, while an action on a bond or recognizance is not.

Secondly. In arresting a defendant on a *ca. sa.*, and he does not immediately pay the debt and costs, he should, forthwith, be committed to the *common jail of the county wherein he is arrested.* The Marshal cannot accept bail, nor can he allow the debtor to go out of the way to procure money wherewith to pay the debt. He must commit him directly to jail; otherwise he may make himself liable as for an escape.

Thirdly. It often happens that a person indicted in one District makes his escape into another. In such case, the Deputy should obtain a *capias* for his arrest, and a certified copy of the indictment to use as evidence. He should then produce the same, and make complaint, before the District Judge of the District where the defendant may be. The Judge will thereupon issue his warrant commanding the Marshal of that District to arrest and bring before him the body of the defendant. The Marshal will either make the arrest himself, or authorize the Deputy to execute the writ. On the prisoner being brought before the Judge, he will, upon proof of identity being furnished, issue his warrant to the Marshal of that District to transport the defendant to the District wherein the offense was committed. And this applies also to detained witnesses. (See act Sept. 24, 1789 1 Stat. at L. 91, § 33.)

The Deputy should then obtain a deputization from the Marshal of that District to transport the prisoner. On making the removal, he should deliver a copy of the warrant to the sheriff or jailer from whose custody the prisoner is taken, and another copy thereof to the sheriff or jailer to whose custody he may be committed, and the original writ, with his return thereon, should be returned to his Marshal.

In some Districts, the Judge issues his warrant for the arrest and transportation of the prisoner directly to the District wherein the offense was committed, without requiring the production of his body before him.

Complaint may also be made before a United States Commissioner, and the same proceedings had as before the Judge, except that the Commissioner must commit the defendant to jail to await the warrant of the Judge for his removal. (For form of Judge's warrant and return thereto, see forms Nos. 66 and 67.)

But the Deputy should, in the first instance, go before the *District Judge* in all cases where it is practicable to do so; and, for that purpose, it would be best to have an indictment previously found, as it will save a great deal of time and expense.

As the Marshal of the foreign District will be entitled to the fees for the arrest and transportation of the prisoner, whether he performs the service or not, the Deputy should require him to sign a disclaimer of all such fees in cases where it is proper to do so. (See form No. 31.)

For any crime or offense against the United States, the offender may, by any Justice or Judge of the United States, or by any justice of the peace or other magistrate of any of the United States, where he may be found (or by any Commissioner of the Circuit Court, act Aug. 23, 1842, 5 Stat. at L. 516, § 1), agreeably to the usual mode of process against offenders in such State, and at the expense of the United States, be arrested and imprisoned or bailed, as the case may be, for trial before such court of the United States as by this act has cognizance of the offense. (Act Sept. 24, 1789, 1 Stat. at L. 91, § 33.)

SECTION IV.

ATTACHMENT.

If a witness subpœnaed on the part of the United States to attend at a term of the Circuit or District Court refuses to attend, an attachment may be procured to compel his attendance. It is only necessary to produce proof of service of the subpœna, and the court will grant an order for attachment, on motion of the District Attorney, — if, upon being called in court, the witness does not appear. It is presumed, however, that, in suits between private parties, the court will require proof of the tender of the legal fees to the witness at the time of serving the subpœna.

In all cases where debts are due from postmasters, mail-contractors or other officers, agents or employees of the post-office department, who are in default or delinquency, a warrant of attachment may issue against all property, real and personal, possessions and rights, legal, equitable and contingent, belonging to such officer and his sureties, or either of them, in the following cases:

1. When any such officer, agent or employee, and his sureties, or either of them, has participated in, aided, abetted or countenanced any rebellion against the United States.

2. When such officer, agent or emyloyee, and his sureties, or either of them, is a non-resident of the District where such officer was appointed, or has departed the District for the purpose of permanently residing elsewhere, or of defrauding the United States, or of avoiding the service of civil process.

3. When such officer or his sureties, or either of them, has conveyed, or is about to convey, or has removed or is about to remove, his property, or any part thereof, from the District with intent to defraud the United States. And where such removal has taken place, certified copies of the warrant may be sent to the Marshal of any other District into which such property may have been removed, under which certified copies, it shall be lawful for such Marshal to seize such property and convey it to some convenient point within the jurisdiction of the court from which the warrant originally issued.

Immediately upon the execution of the warrant of attachment, the Marshal shall cause due publication of such attachment to be made, in the case of absconding debtors or adherents of the rebellion, for two months, and in case of non-residents for four months. Such publication to be made in some newspaper or newspapers within the District where the property attached is situated, and the details of such publication shall be regulated in each case by the order under which the warrant is issued.

GENERAL INFORMATION. 33

When any person or persons indebted to or having possession of the property of such defendants, or either of them, shall be known to the District Attorney or the Marshal, it shall be the duty of such officer to see that personal notice of such attachment is served upon such persons, as in cases of garnishees.

The fees, costs and expenses of issuing and serving the warrant of attachment shall be regulated as far as possible by the existing laws of the United States and the rules of court made in pursuance thereof. (Act Feb. 23, 1865, 13 Stat. at L. 432.)

SECTION V.

BAIL.

The subject of arrest and bail in the United States Courts is regulated and governed by the local law in each District.

As a general rule, bail should reside within the jurisdiction of the court before whom the prisoner is acknowledged to appear, — or before whom the suit or proceeding, wherein bail is offered, shall be pending.

Any party charged with a criminal offense, and admitted to bail, may, in vacation, be arrested by his bail and delivered to the Marshal or his Deputy, before any Judge or other officer having power to commit for such offense; and, at the request of such bail, the Judge or other officer shall recommit the party so arrested to the custody of the Marshal, and indorse on the recognizance, or certified copy thereof, the discharge and *exoneratur* of such bail; and the party so committed shall therefrom be held in custody until discharged by due course of law. (Act Aug. 8, 1846, 9 Stat. at L. 73, § 4.)

Upon all arrests in criminal cases, bail shall be admitted, except where the punishment may be death, in which cases, it shall not be admitted, but by the Supreme or a Circuit Court, or by a Justice of the Supreme Court, or a Judge of a District Court, who shall exercise their discretion therein, regarding the nature and circumstances of the offense, and of the evidence and the usages of law. And if a person committed by a Justice of the Supreme or a Judge of a District Court, for an offense not punishable with death, shall afterward procure bail, and there be no Judge of the United States in the District to take the same, it may be taken by any Judge of the Supreme or Superior Court of law of such State. (Act Sept. 24, 1789, 1 Stat. at L. 91, § 33.)

Bail for appearance in any court of the United States, in any criminal cause in which bail is by law allowed, may be taken by any Judge of the United States, any Chancellor, Judge of a Supreme or Superior Court, or chief or first Judge of any Court of Common Pleas of any State, or mayor of a city in either of them, and by any person having authority from a Circuit Court, to take bail; which authority, revocable at the discretion of such court, any Circuit Court may give to one or more discreet persons, learned in the law, in any District for which such court is holden, where, from the extent of the District, and remoteness of its parts from the usual residence of any of the before-named officers, such provision shall, in the opinion of the court, be necessary: *Provided*, that nothing herein shall be construed to extend to taking bail in any case where the punishment for the offense may be death; nor to abridge any power heretofore given by the laws of the United States to any description of persons to take bail. (Act March 2, 1793, 1 Stat. at L. 334, § 4.)

Upon the necessary proof being made to any Judge of the United States, or other magistrate having authority to commit on criminal charges against the laws of the United States, that a person previously admitted to bail on any such criminal charge is about to abscond, and that his bail is insufficient, it shall and may be lawful for any such Judge or magistrate to require such person to give better security, or, for default thereof, to cause him to be committed to prison; and, to that end, an order for his arrest may be indorsed on the former commitment, or a new warrant therefor may be issued by such Judge or magistrate, setting forth the cause thereof. (Act Aug. 8, 1846, 9 Stat. at L. 73, § 6.)

The Clerks of the District and Circuit Courts, in the absence or in case of the disability of the judges, are authorized "to take recognizances of special bail, *de bene esse*, in any action depending in either of the said courts. (Act May 8, 1792, 1 Stat. at L. 278, § 10.)

The Judges of the Supreme Court, and of the several District Courts of the United States, and all Judges and Justices of the courts of the several States, having authority by the laws of the United

States to take cognizance of offenses against the Constitution and laws thereof (and also the Commissioners of the Circuit Court, act May 15, 1862, 12 Stat. at L. 387, § 8), shall respectively have the like power and authority to hold to security of the peace and for good behavior, in cases arising under the Constitution and laws of the United States, as may or can be lawfully exercised by any Judge or Justice of the peace of the respective States, in cases cognizable before them. (Act July 16, 1798, 1 Stat. at L. 609, § 1.)

In all cases where a defendant, who hath procured bail to respond the judgment in a suit brought against him in any of the courts of the United States, shall afterwards be arrested in any District of the United States, other than that in which the first suit was brought, and shall be committed to a gaol, the use of which shall have been ceded to the United States for the custody of prisoners, it shall be lawful for and the duty of any Judge of the Court in which the suit is depending, wherein such defendant had so procured bail as aforesaid, at the request and for the indemnification of the bail, to order and direct that such defendant be held in the gaol to which he shall have been committed a prisoner, in the custody of the Marshal, within whose district such gaol is, and upon the said order duly authenticated being delivered to the said Marshal, it shall be his duty to receive such prisoner into his custody, and him safely to keep, and the Marshal shall thereupon be chargeable, as in other cases, for an escape. And the said Marshal thereupon shall make a certificate, under his hand and seal, of such commitment, and transmit the same to the court from which such order issued; and shall also, if required, make a duplicate thereof, and deliver the same to such bail, his or their agent or attorney, and upon the said certificate being returned to the Court which made the said order, it shall be lawful for the said Court or any Judge thereof, to direct that an *exoneratur* be entered upon the bail piece where special bail shall have been found, or otherwise to discharge such bail, and such bail shall thereupon accordingly be discharged.

§ 2. The Marshal or his Deputy, serving such order as aforesaid, shall therefor receive the same fees and allowances as for the service of an original process commitment thereon to the gaol and the return thereof.

§ 3. In every case of commitment as aforesaid, by virtue of such order as aforesaid, the person so committed shall, unless sooner discharged by law, be holden in gaol until final judgment shall be rendered in the suit in which he procured bail as aforesaid, and sixty days thereafter, if such judgment shall be rendered against him, that he may be charged in execution, which may be directed to and served by the Marshal in whose custody he is. (Act March 2, 1799, 1 Stat. at L. 727.) See "Affidavits and Depositions."

SECTION VI.

DISTRESS WARRANTS.

If any collector of the revenue, receiver of public money, or other officer who shall have received the public money before it is paid into the treasury of the United States, shall fail to render his account, or pay over the same in the manner or within the time required by law, it shall be the duty of the first comptroller of the treasury to cause to be stated the account of such collector, receiver of public money or other officer, exhibiting truly the amount due to the United States, and certify the same to the [Solicitor of the Treasury, act May 29, 1830, 4 Stat. at L. 414, § 1], who is hereby authorized and required to issue a warrant of distress against such delinquent officer and his sureties, directed to the Marshal of the District in which such delinquent officer and his surety or sureties shall reside, and where the said officer and his surety or sureties shall reside in different Districts, or where they, or either of them shall reside in a District other than that in which the estate of either may be situate, which may be intended to be taken and sold, then such warrant shall be directed to the Marshals of such Districts, and to their Deputies respectively; therein specifying the amount with which such delinquent is chargeable, and the sums, if any, which have been paid. And the Marshal authorized to execute such warrant shall, by himself or by his Deputy, proceed to levy and collect the sum remaining due, by distress and sale of the goods and chattels of such delinquent officer; having given ten days' previous notice of such intended sale, by affixing an advertisement of the articles to be sold at two or more public places in the town and county where the said goods or chattels were taken, or in the town or county where the owner of such goods or chattels may reside; and if the goods and chattels be not sufficient to satisfy the said warrant, the same may be levied upon the person of such officer, who may be committed to prison, there to remain until discharged by due course of law. Notwithstanding the commitment of such officer, or if he abscond, or if goods and chattels cannot be found sufficient to satisfy the said warrant, the Marshal or his Deputy may and shall proceed to levy and collect the sum which remains due by such delinquent officer, by the distress and sale of the goods and chattels of the surety or sureties of such officer; having given ten days' previous notice of such intended sale, by affixing an advertisement of the articles to be sold at two or more public places in the town or county where the said goods or chattels were taken, or in the town or county where the owner of such goods or chattels resides. And the amount due by any such officer as aforesaid shall be, and the same is hereby declared to be, a lien upon the lands, tenements and hereditaments of such officer and his sureties, from the date of a levy in pursuance of the warrant of distress issued against him or them, and a record thereof made in the office of the Clerk of the District Court of the proper District, until th same shall be discharged according to law. And for want of goods and chattels of such officer, or his surety or sureties, sufficient to satisfy any warrant of distress issued pursuant to the provisions of this act, the lands, tenements and hereditaments of such officer and his surety or sureties, or so much thereof as may be necessary for that purpose, after being advertised for at least three weeks in not less than three public places in the county or District where such real estate is situate, prior to the time of sale, may and shall be sold by the Marshal of such District or his Deputy; and for all lands, tenements or hereditaments sold in pursuance of the authority aforesaid, the conveyance of the Marshals or their Deputies, executed in due form of law, shall give a valid title against all persons claiming under such delinquent officer, or his surety or sureties. And all moneys which may remain of the proceeds of such sales, after satisfying the said warrant of distress and paying the reasonable costs and charges of the sale, shall be returned to such delinquent officer or surety as the case may be. (Act May 15, 1820; 3 Stat. at L. 592, § 2.)

Disbursing officers in the civil, military and naval departments of the government of the United States, and their sureties, are included in the provisions of the preceding section, and to the same extent, as if they had been described and enumerated in the said section. (Id. § 3.)

If any person should consider himself aggrieved by any warrant issued under this act, he may prefer a bill of complaint to any District Judge of the United States, setting forth therein the nature and extent of the injury of which he complains; and thereupon the Judge aforesaid may, if in his opinion the case requires it, grant an injunction to stay proceedings on such warrant altogether, or for so much thereof as the nature of the case requires; but no injunction shall issue till the party applying for the same shall give bond, and sufficient security, conditioned for the performance of such judgment as shall be awarded against the complainant, in such amount as the Judge granting the injunction shall prescribe; nor shall the issuing of such injunction in any manner impair the lien produced by the issuing of such warrant. And the same proceedings shall be had on such injunction as in other cases, except that no answer shall be necessary on the part of the United States; and if, upon dissolving the injunction, it shall appear, to the satisfaction of the Judge who shall decide upon the same, that the application for the injunction was merely for delay, in addition to the lawful interest which shall be assessed on all sums which may be found due against the complainant, the said Judge is hereby authorized to add such damages as that, with the lawful interest, it shall not exceed the rate of ten per centum per annum on the principal sum. (Id. § 4.)

Such injunction may be granted or dissolved by such Judge, either in or out of court. (Id. § 5.)

The above act does not apply to every commissioned officer of the army or navy, to whose hands any public money may be intrusted, but only to those regularly appointed disbursing officers, who may have given official bonds, with sureties, for the faithful performance of their duties. (*Ex parte Randolph*, 2 Brock. Marsh. 448.)

The warrant issued by the Solicitor of the Treasury is conclusive evidence of the facts recited in it, and of the authority to make the levy, so far as to justify the Marshal in making it. (*Murray's Lessee* v. *Hoboken Land and Improvement Co.*, 18 How. 272.)

It is not inconsistent with the Constitution of the United States. (Ibid.)

It is not recollected that in the Northern District of New York, any action has ever been had under the foregoing statute, and it is questionable whether any reference to such a summary mode of proceeding should here be made. But, as by the ninth section of the act it is provided that nothing in said act contained "shall be construed to take away or impair any right or remedy which the United States now have, by law, for the recovery of debts or demands," and as in the Northern District of New York the practice has been, and now is, to institute an action on the bond of the delinquent officer, to recover the penalty thereof, it would seem that it is in the discretion of the Solicitor of the Treasury to issue a warrant of distress, or to institute an ordinary action on the bond, for the recovery of the penalty.

For form of the solicitor's warrant, see form No. 68. By reference to forms Nos. 55, 64 and 65, the Deputy Marshal will have no difficulty in making out the proper return.

GENERAL INFORMATION. 43

SECTION VII.

EXECUTION.

Where it is now required by the laws of any State, that goods taken in execution on a writ of *fieri facias* shall be appraised previous to the sale thereof, it shall be lawful for the appraisers appointed under the authority of the State to appraise goods taken in execution on a *fieri facias* issued out of any court of the United States, in the same manner as if such writ had issued out of a court held under the authority of the State ; and it shall be the duty of the Marshal, in whose custody such goods may be, to summon the appraisers in like manner as the sheriff is by the laws of the State required to summon them ; and the appraisers shall be entitled to the like fees as in cases of appraisement under the laws of the State ; and if the appraisers, being duly summoned, shall fail to attend and perform the duties required of them, the Marshal may proceed to sell such goods, without an appraisement. (Act March 2, 1793, 1 Stat. at L. 335, § 8.)

Writs of execution, and other final process issued on judgments and decrees rendered in any of the courts of the United States, and the proceedings thereupon, shall be the same, except their style, in each State respectively, as are now used in the courts of such State, saving to the courts of the United States in those States in which there are not courts of equity, with the ordinary equity jurisdiction, the power of prescribing the mode of executing their decrees in equity, by rules of court: *Provided, however,* that it shall be in the power of the courts, if they see fit, in their discretion, by rules of court, so far to alter final process in said courts as to conform the same to any change which may be adopted by the Legislatures of the respective States for the State courts. (Act May 19, 1828, 4 Stat. at L. 281, § 3.)

Pursuant to the provisions contained in the foregoing section, the District Court for the Northern District of New York has heretofore made the following rule, viz.:

" In all cases not provided for by the rules of this court, or by law, the practice of the Supreme Court of this State, as prescribed by the Revised Statutes of this State, and by the rules of the said court, shall regulate the practice of this court, so far as the same may be applicable." (Rule 83.)

By Rule VI, of the Circuit Court for said District, the above rule has also been adopted by that court.

From this it will readily be seen that the "Exemption Laws" of the several States are applicable to executions issued out of the courts of the United States, there being no law of the United States on that subject.

If property is seized under a *fieri facias*, before the return day of the writ, the Marshal may proceed to sell at any time afterwards, without any new process from the court: as a special return on the *fieri facias* is one of the necessary modes of proving the sale, the Marshal must be authorized to make the indorsement after the regular return term, in cases where

GENERAL INFORMATION. 45

the sale was made afterwards. (*Remington* v. *Linthicum*, 14 Pet. 84.)

All writs of execution upon any judgment obtained for the use of the United States, in any of the courts of the United States in one State, may run and be executed in any other State, or in any of the territories of the United States, but shall be issued from, and made returnable to the court where the judgment was obtained, any law to the contrary notwithstanding. (Act March 3, 1797, 1 Stat. at L. 515, § 6.)

All writs of execution, upon any judgment or decree, obtained in any of the District or Circuit Courts of the United States, in any one State, which shall have been, or may hereafter be, divided into two Judicial Districts, may run and be executed in any part of such State; but shall be issued from, and made returnable to, the court where the judgment was obtained, any law to the contrary notwithstanding. (Act May 20, 1826; 4 Stat. at L. 184.)

A Marshal's sale of land on execution, where the defendant had no interest in the land, will be set aside on motion.

In such sale, there is no warranty by the defendant. The purchaser must understand what he buys.

But where he has been deceived or misinformed, the court will release him by setting aside the sale. This is a proper mode of giving relief, if application be made before the sale shall be completed. (*Rocksell* v. *Allen*, 3 McL. 357.)

Whenever a Marshal shall sell any lands, tenements or hereditaments by virtue of process from a court of the United States, and shall die, or be removed from office, or the term of his commission expires, before a deed shall be executed for the same by him to the purchaser; in every such case, the purchaser or plaintiff, at whose suit the sale was made, may apply to the court from which the process issued, and set forth the case, assigning the reason why the title was not perfected by the Marshal who sold the same; and thereupon the court may order the Marshal for the time being to perfect the title and execute a deed to the purchaser, he paying the purchase-money and costs remaining unpaid; and where a Marshal shall take in execution any lands, tenements or hereditaments, and shall die, or be removed from office, or the term of his commission expires before sale, or other final disposition made of the same; in every such case, the like process shall issue to the succeeding Marshal, and the same proceedings shall be had, as if such former Marshal had not died or been removed, or the term of his commission had not expired. (Act May 7, 1800, 2 Stat. at L. 61, § 3.)

The two last clauses of the above section — in connection with the act of September 24, 1789; 1 Stat. at L. 87, § 28 (see page 74) — have given rise to various and conflicting decisions as to whether or not, in cases where a Marshal has made a levy, and shall die, or be removed from office, or the term of his commission expires before sale, he, or his Deputy, can lawfully proceed to sell the property.

In the case of *McFarland* v. *Gwin*, 1845 (3 How. 720), Justice McKinley, in delivering the opinion of the court, said:

"It is a well settled principle of law, that, if an execution come to the hands of a sheriff to be executed, and his term of office expires before he executes it, he is bound nevertheless to complete the execution; and the same rule applies to a Marshal. An execution is never completed until the money is made and paid over to the plaintiff, if it be practicable to make it."

And in the case of *Doolittle's Lessee* v. *Bryan*, 1852 (14 How. 563), which was certified for decision from the Circuit Court for the District of Ohio, the Supreme Court there gave it as their opinion, " That a sale of land by a Marshal, on a *venditioni exponas*, after he is removed from office, and a new Marshal appointed and qualified, is not void." Justice Grier delivered the opinion of the court, and remarked: "There is no express repeal of the act of 1789 to be found in this act of 1800. Nor does it contain any negative terms which are necessarily contrary to the previous affirmative act. A latter act is never construed to repeal a prior act unless there be a contrariety or repugnancy in them, or at least some notice taken of the former act so as to vindicate an intention to repeal it. The law does not favor a repeal by implication, unless the repugnance be quite plain; hence it has been decided, that, although two acts of parliament be seemingly repugnant, yet, if there be no clause of *non obstante* in the latter, they shall, if possible, have such a construction that the latter may not be a repeal of the former by implication." *

" The purview of the clause of the act of 1789, now in question, is to define the powers of a Marshal having process in his hands at the time he is removed or his office expires; it authorizes him to execute process previously directed to him. The act of 1800 is evidently intended to confer rights on the parties to have the same acts performed by the new Marshal. It gives cumulative rights and powers for the benefit of suitors."

It has, however, been decided that the Marshal *cannot* sell property after his removal from office or the expiration of his commission, even though a levy has been made. (See *Bowerbank* v. *Morris*, 1801, Wall. C. Ct. 118; *Overton* v. *Gorham*, 1841, 2 McL. 509; *Stewart* v. *Hamilton*, 1849, 4 id. 534; and *U. S.* v. *Bank of Arkansas*, 1846, Hempst. 460.)

The opinions *in favor* of the sale by a Marshal on execution after his removal from office, or the expiration of his commission, it will be seen were given by the Supreme Court of the United States, while the decisions *against* it were rendered in several of the Circuit Courts.

In conclusion, the law laid down in *McFarland* v. *Gwin*, and *Doolittle's Lessee* v. *Bryan*, are, as a matter of course, entitled to the greater consideration as emanating from the highest court of the Union; and also from the further fact that the former case is the latest decision on the subject, and reviews in a general way all prior cases. It may, therefore, with safety be said that, when a Marshal shall be removed from office, or his commission expires, he may execute and return all process remaining in his hands at the time of his removal or the expiration of his commission; and, in case he shall die, then that his Deputies may execute and return the same. And this includes the sale of property on execution, on which a levy has been made, as well as the service of all other process.

GENERAL INFORMATION. 49

SECTION VIII.

EXTRADITION.

By section 1, act of Aug. 12, 1848 (9 Stat. at L. 302, § 1), the Justices of the Supreme Court, and Judges of the several District Courts of the United States, and the Judges of the several State courts, and the Commissioners authorized so to do by any of the courts of the United States, are authorized to hear and decide cases under the act for the extradition of foreign criminals.

Where a court of one of the States assumes to take, by *habeas corpus*, out of the hands of the Marshal of the United States, a person held by him as a fugitive from crime committed in a foreign country, and under reclamation by treaty, it is the right of the Marshal to refuse to have the body of the party before the State court, and it is the duty of the courts and other authorities of the United States to protect the Marshal in such refusal by all means known to the law. (6 Op. Atty.-Gen. 237.)

Where a Marshal of the United States has in custody a fugitive from foreign justice, under warrant of extradition from the proper authorities of the United States, and a State court undertakes to usurp jurisdiction of the case, it is the duty of the Marshal, disregarding any process of the State court, to take the party to the exterior line of such State, and there deliver him to the agent of the foreign government. (6 Op. Atty.-Gen. 290.)

A person not conveyed out of the United States within two calendar months after commitment for extradition, over and above the time actually required to convey the prisoner from the jail to which he or she may have been committed, by the readiest way, out of the United States, it shall be lawful for any Judge of the United States, or of any State, upon application made to him, and upon proof that reasonable notice of the intention to make such application has been given to the Secretary of State, to order the person so committed to be discharged out of custody, unless sufficient cause shall be shown to such Judge why such discharge ought not to be ordered. (Act Aug. 12, 1848, 9 Stat. at L. 303, § 4.)

The ordinary expenses attending the process of international extradition are to be defrayed by the demanding government. (7 Op. Atty.-Gen. 612, 396; 9 id. 497.)

"Whenever any person who shall have been delivered by any foreign government to an agent or agents of the United States, for the purpose of being brought within the United States and tried for any crime of which he is duly accused, the President shall have power to take all necessary measures for the transportation and safe keeping of such accused person, and for his security against lawless violence, until the final conclusion of his trial for the crime[s] or offenses specified in the warrant of extradition, and until his final discharge from custody or imprisonment for or on account of such crimes or offenses, and for a reasonable time thereafter. And it shall be lawful for the President, or such person as he may empower for that purpose, to employ such portion of the land or naval forces of the United States, or of the militia thereof, as may be necessary for the safe keeping and protection of the accused as aforesaid.

"SECTION 2. *And be it further enacted*, That any person duly appointed as agent to receive in behalf of the United States the delivery by a foreign government of any person accused of crime committed within the jurisdiction of the United States, and to convey him to the place of his trial, shall be, and hereby is, vested with all the powers of a Marshal of the United States, in the several Districts 'through which it may be necessary for him to pass with such prisoner, so far as such power is requisite for his safe keeping.

"SECTION 3. *And be it further enacted*, That, if any person or persons shall knowingly and willfully obstruct, resist or oppose such agent in the execution of his duties, or shall rescue, or attempt to rescue, such prisoner, whether in the custody of the agent aforesaid, or of any Marshal, sheriff, jailer or other officer, or person to whom his custody may have lawfully been committed, every person so knowingly and willfully offending in the premises shall, on conviction thereof before the District or Circuit Court of the United States for the District in which the offense was committed, be fined not exceeding one thousand dollars, and imprisoned not exceeding one year." (Act March 3, 1869, 3 Pamphlet Laws, 1868–9, 337.)

SECTION IX.

FEES.

For Attorneys', Clerks', Marshals', Jurors', Witnesses' Printers and Commissioners' fees, see *Appendix* (A.)

A Marshal of the United States is entitled to compensation for serving a subpœna in a criminal case on a witness beyond the limits of his own District, and also for executing an attachment on the same witness for failing to appear. (9 Op. Atty.-Gen. 265.)

Marshals are entitled to compensation for transporting witnesses in custody, though it be not mentioned by the statute, by analogy of the statute compensation for the transportation of criminals. (6 Op. Atty.-Gen. 58.)

Where a Marshal received, in due course of law, process of summons and subpœna for the same witnesses (it being the usual mode of procuring the attendance of witnesses in the court from which they issued), and served the same as required, he is entitled to his fees for both services, on their being allowed and certified by the District Judge. (3 Op. Atty.-Gen. 496.)

"Before the accounts of the United States Marshals, District Attorneys and Clerks are presented to the accounting officers of the Treasury Department for settlement, they shall be examined and certified to by the District Judge of the United States in the District in which the officers presenting the accounts officiate, whether in the States or Territories, and the same shall be subject to revision upon their merits by said accounting officers, as in case of other public accounts : *Provided, however,* that no accounts of fees or costs paid to any witness or juror, upon the order of any Judge or Commissioner, shall be so re-examined as to charge any Marshal for an erroneous taxation of such fees or costs." (Act Aug. 16, 1856, 11 Stat. at L. 49, § 1.)

An appeal lies from the decision of the accounting officers to the Secretary of the Interior. (Id. § 4.)

SECTION X.

INDICTMENT.

No person shall be held to answer for a capital or otherwise infamous crime, unless on a presentment or indictment of a Grand Jury, except in cases arising in the land or naval forces, or in the militia, when in actual service, in time of war or public danger; nor shall any person be subject for the same offense to be twice put in jeopardy of life or limb.* (Art V. Amendments to United States Constitution.)

Indictments for all offenses against the United States may be found indifferently, either in the District or Circuit Court, and may, at the instance of the District Attorney, by order of the court having possession of them, be transmitted from the one court to the other for trial, except that all indictments for capital offenses found in either court are triable only in the Circuit Court, whither it is made the duty of the

54   GENERAL INFORMATION.

District Court to send all such indictments found therein. (Act Aug. 8, 1846; 9 Stat. at L. 72, §§ 2, 3.)

No indictment shall be found, nor shall any presentment be made, without the concurrence of at least twelve Grand Jurors. (Act March 3, 1865, 13 Stat. at L. 500, § 1.)

Whenever there are or shall be several charges against any person or persons for the same act or transaction, or for two or more acts or transactions connected together, or for two or more acts or transactions of the same class of crimes or offenses, which may be properly joined, instead of having several indictments, the whole may be joined in one indictment in separate counts; and if two or more indictments shall be found in such cases, the court may order them consolidated. (Act Feb. 26, 1853, 10 Stat. at L. 162.)

SECTION XI

INTEREST.

On all judgments in civil cases, recovered in the Circuit or District Courts, interest is allowed, and may be levied by the Marshal, under process of execution issued thereon, in all cases where, by the law of the State in which such Circuit or District Court shall be held, interest may be levied, under process of execution, on judgments recovered in the courts of such State, to be calculated from the date of the judgment, and at such rate per annum as is allowed by law on judgments recovered in the courts of such State. (Act Aug. 23, 1842, 5 Stat. at L. 518, § 8.)

SECTION XII

IMPRISONMENT FOR DEBT.

No person shall be imprisoned for debt in any State, on process issuing out of a court of the United States, where, by the laws of such State, imprisonment for debt has been abolished; and where, by the laws of a State, imprisonment for debt shall be allowed, under certain conditions and restrictions, the same conditions and restrictions shall be applicable to the process issuing out of the courts of the United States; and the same proceedings shall be had therein as are adopted in the courts of such State. (Act Feb. 28, 1839, 5 Stat. at L. 321, § 1.)

The above provision is to be "so construed as to abolish imprisonment for debt on process issuing out of any court of the United States, in all cases whatever, where, by the laws of the State in which the court shall be held, imprisonment for debt has been, or shall hereafter be, abolished." (Act Jan. 14, 1841, 5 Stat. at L. 410, § 1.)

Imprisonment for debt is abolished in all cases, where, by the laws of the State, it has been or shall be abolished, " upon similar or analogous process issuing from a State court;" that is, if a defendant in the State courts is exempt from personal arrest and imprisonment on all process, whether mesne or final, in cases sounding in contract, then the defendant in *admiralty* will, in all such cases, be, in like manner, exempt. (*The Kentucky*, 4 Blatch. C. C. 450.)

Whenever, upon mesne process or execution issuing out of any of the courts of the United States, any defendant therein is arrested or imprisoned, he shall be entitled to discharge from such arrest or imprisonment in the same manner as if he was so arrested or imprisoned on like process of the State courts in the same District. And the same oath may be taken, and the same length of notice thereof shall be required, as is provided by such State laws; and all modifications, conditions and restrictions upon imprisonment for debt, now existing by the laws of any State, shall be applicable to process issuing out of the courts of the United States therein, and the same course of proceedings shall be adopted as now are or may be in the courts of such States. But all such proceedings shall be had before some one of the Commissioners appointed by the United States Circuit Court to take bail and affidavits. (Act March 2, 1867, 14 Stat. at L. 543.)

SECTION XIII.

JAILS.

On the 3d day of March, 1791 (1 Stat. at L. 225), after reciting that it had theretofore been recommended to the several States to pass laws making it expressly the duty of the keepers of their jails to receive and safe keep therein all prisoners committed under the authority of the United States; and, in order to insure the administration of justice, Congress did thereupon resolve,

"That in case any State shall not have complied with the said recommendation, the Marshal in such State, under the direction of the Judge of the District, be authorized to hire a convenient place to serve as a temporary jail, and to make the necessary provision for the safe-keeping of prisoners committed under the authority of the United States, until permanent provision shall be made by law for that purpose; and the said Marshal shall be allowed his reasonable expenses incurred for the above purposes, to be paid out of the treasury of the United States." By a resolution passed March 3, 1821 (3 Stat. at L. 646), this provision was extended to all cases in which any State or States, having complied with the aforementioned recommendation, "shall have withdrawn, or shall hereafter withdraw, either in whole or in part, the use of their jails for prisoners committed under the authority of the United States."

And by a further provision of law it was enacted, "That in any State where the jails are not allowed to be used for the imprisonment of persons arrested or committed under the laws of the United States, or where houses are not allowed to be so used, it shall and may be lawful for any Marshal, under the direction of the Judge of the United States for the proper District, to use other convenient places, within the limits of said State, and to make such other provision as he may deem expedient and necessary for that purpose." (Act March 2, 1833, 4 Stat. at L. 634, § 6.)

All persons who have been, or who may hereafter be convicted of crime by any court of the United States (not military), the punishment whereof shall be imprisonment, in a District or Territory where, at the time of such conviction, there may be no penitentiary or other prison suitable for the confinement of convicts of the United States, and available therefor, shall be confined during the term for which they have been or may be sentenced, in some suitable prison in a convenient State or Territory to be designated by the Secretary of the Interior, and shall be transported and delivered to the warden or keeper of the prison by the Marshal of the District or Territory where such conviction shall have occurred; * * the reasonable actual expense of transportation, necessary subsistence and hire, and transportation of guards and the Marshal, * * only, to be paid by the Secretary of the Interior out of the judiciary fund: *Provided*, that if, in the opinion of the Secretary, the expense of transportation from any State or Territory * * in which there is no penitentiary will exceed the cost of maintaining them in jail in the State or Territory * * during the period of their sentence, then it shall be lawful so to confine them therein for the period designated in their sentence. (Act May 12, 1864, 13 Stat. at L. 74, § 1.)

SECTION XIV.

JUDGMENTS.

"That judgments and decrees hereafter rendered in the Circuit and District Courts of the United States, within any State, shall cease to be liens on real estate or chattels real in the same manner and at

GENERAL INFORMATION. 59

like periods as judgments and decrees of the courts of such State now cease by law to be liens thereon." (Act July 4, 1840, 5 Stat. at L. 393, § 4.)

In all criminal cases in which there has been or shall be a judgment or sentence against any person, as a fine or penalty, whether alone or along with any other kind of punishment, the same shall be deemed a judgment debt, and (unless pardoned or remitted by the President) may be collected on execution in the common form of law. (Act Feb. 20, 1863, 12 Stat. at L. 657, § 2.)

When a Sheriff first levies on personal property, under a State judgment, there is a prior lien, over a levy subsequently made on the same property by the Marshal. (*Earl* v. *Raymond*, 4 McL. 233.)

A judgment against one of the partners of a firm, will authorize the sheriff or Marshal to levy on the interest of the judgment debtor in the goods. (*U. S.* v. *B. O. Williams*, id. 236.)

SECTION XV.

JURIES.

"Every Grand Jury impaneled before any District or Circuit Court of the United States, to inquire into and presentment make of public offenses against the United States, committed or triable within the District for which the court is holden, shall consist of not less than sixteen and not exceeding twenty-three persons. If, of the persons summoned, less than sixteen attend, they shall be placed on the Grand Jury, and the court shall order the Marshal to summon, either immediately or for a day fixed, from the body of the District, and not from the bystanders, a sufficient number of persons to complete the Grand Jury. And whenever a challenge to an individual grand juror is allowed, and there are not other jurors in attendance, sufficient to complete the Grand Jury, the court shall make a like order to the Marshal to summon a sufficient number of persons for that purpose. No indictment shall be found, nor shall any presentment be made, without the concurrence of at least twelve grand jurors. From the persons summoned and accepted as grand jurors, the court shall appoint the foreman, who shall have power to administer oaths and affirmations to witnesses appearing before the Grand Jury." (Act March 3, 1865, 13 Stat. at L. 500, § 1.)

When the offense charged be treason or a capital offense, the defendant shall be entitled to twenty and the United States to five peremptory challenges. On a trial for any other offense in which the right of peremptory challenge now exists, the defendant shall be entitled to ten and the United States to two peremptory challenges. All challenges, whether to the array or panel, or to individual jurors for cause or favor, shall be tried by the court without the aid of triers. (Id. § 2.)

And in all trials in capital cases, if the party indicted shall peremptorily challenge above the number of jurors allowed by law, such excess of challenges shall be disallowed by the court, and the cause shall proceed for trial in the same manner as if the same challenges had not been made. (Act March 3, 1835, 4 Stat. at L. 777, § 4.)

By an act entitled "An act to provide for the summary trial of minor offenses against the laws of the United States," if the trial of a complaint for any offense therein mentioned be had before a jury, the United States and the accused shall each be entitled to three peremptory challenges. Challenges for cause, in such cases, shall be tried by the court without the aid of triers. (Act June 11, 1864, 13 Stat. at L. 125, § 7.)

In addition to the existing causes of disqualification and challenge of grand and petit jurors in the courts of the United States, the following are hereby declared and established, namely: Without duress and coercion to have taken up arms or to have joined any insurrection and rebellion against the United States; to have adhered to any rebellion, giving it aid and comfort; to have given, directly or indirectly, any assistance, in money, arms, horses, clothes or anything whatever, to or for the use or benefit of any person or persons whom the person giving such assistance knew to have joined, or to be about to join, any insurrection or rebellion, or to have resisted, or to be about to resist with force of arms, the execution of the laws of the United States, or who, he had good ground to believe, had joined, or was about to join, any insurrection or rebellion, or had resisted or was about to resist, with force of arms, the execution of the laws of the United States; and to have counseled and advised any person or persons to join any insurrection and rebellion, or to resist with force of arms the laws of the United States. (Act June 17, 1862, 12 Stat. at L. 430, § 1.)

Jurors to serve in the courts of the United States, in each State respectively, shall have the like qualifications, and be entitled to the like exemptions, as jurors of the highest court of law of such State now have and are entitled to, and shall hereafter from time to time have and be entitled to ; and shall be designated by ballot, lot or otherwise, according to the mode of forming such juries now practiced and hereafter to be practiced therein, in so far as such mode may be practicable by the courts of the United States, or the officers thereof ; and for this purpose the said courts shall have power to make all necessary rules and regulations for conforming the designation and impaneling of juries, in substance, to the laws and usages now in force in such State ; and further, shall have power, by rule or order, from time to time, to conform the same to any change in these respects which may be hereafter adopted by the Legislatures of the respective States for the State courts. (Act July 20, 1840, 5 Stat. at L. 394, § 1.)

* * "And shall be returned, as there shall be occasion for them, from such parts of the District, from time to time, as the court shall direct, so as shall be most favorable to an impartial trial, and so as not to incur an unnecessary expense, or unduly to burden the citizens of any part of the District with such services. And writs of *venire facias*, when directed by the court, shall issue from the clerk's office, and shall be served and returned by the Marshal in his proper person or by his Deputy, or, in case the Marshal or his Deputy is not an indifferent person, or is interested in the event of the cause, by such fit person as the court shall specially appoint for that purpose, to whom they shall administer an oath or affirmation that he will truly and impartially serve and return such writ." * * * (Act Sept. 24, 1789, 1 Stat. at L. 88, § 29.)

Jurors to serve in the courts of the United States shall be designated by lot or otherwise, in each State or District respectively, according to the mode of forming juries to serve in the highest courts of law therein now practiced; so far as the same shall render such designation, practicable by the courts and Marshals of the United States. (Act May 13, 1800, 2 Stat. at L, 82, § 1.)

This provision of the law is in force in the State of Pennsylvania only.

On completing the panels, the Deputy Marshal should send a copy thereof to the clerk of the court for which they are drawn, and a copy of the list of *grand jurors* to the United States Attorney of his District.

In the Northern District of New York the jurors are required to be summoned at least six days previous to the holding of the court, by giving personal notice to each person, or by leaving a written notice at his place of residence, with some person of suitable age. (See form No. 43.)

SECTION XVI.

LIMITATION.

"No person shall be prosecuted, tried, or punished for the capital offenses [treason, murder, piracy, and casting away vessels] set forth in the act to which this act is in addition (act April 30, 1790, 1 Stat. at L. 119, § 32; act March 26, 1804, 2 Stat. at L. 290, §§ 1, 2), unless the indictment for the same is found by a grand jury within five years after such capital offense is committed." (Act July 25, 1868, 2 Pamphlet Laws, 1867-8, 183, § 1.)

"This act shall take effect from and after its passage, and its provisions shall be applicable equally to offenses committed within three years before and offenses committed after its passage. (Id. § 2.)

* * "Nor shall any person be prosecuted, tried or punished for any offense not capital, * * unless the indictment * * for the same shall be found or instituted within two years from the time of committing the offense. * * *Provided*, that nothing herein contained shall extend to any person or persons fleeing from justice." (Act April 30, 1790, 1 Stat. at L. 119, § 32.)

No suit or prosecution shall be maintained for any penalty or forfeiture, pecuniary or otherwise, accruing under the laws of the United States, unless the same suit or prosecution shall be commenced within five years from the time when the penalty or forfeiture accrued. *Provided*, the person of the offender or the property liable for such penalty or forfeiture shall, within the same period, be found within the United States, so that the proper process may be instituted and served against such person or property therefor. (Act Feb. 28, 1839, 5 Stat. at L. 322, § 4.)

"That the time for finding indictments in the courts of the United States in the late rebel States for offenses cognizable by said courts, and which may have been committed since said States went into rebellion, be, and hereby is, extended for the period of two years from and after [the time when] said States are or may be restored to representation in Congress: *Provided, however*, that the provisions hereof shall not apply to treason or other political offenses." (Act March 3, 1869, 3 Pamphlet Laws 1868-9, 340.)

"No suit or prosecution, civil or criminal, shall be maintained for any arrest or imprisonment made, or other trespasses or wrongs done or committed, or act omitted to be done, at any time during the present rebellion, by virtue or under color of any authority derived from or exercised by or under the President of the United States, or by or under any act of Congress, unless the same shall have been commenced within two years next after such arrest, imprisonment, trespass or wrong may have been done or committed, or act may have been omitted to be done: *Provided*, that in no case shall the limitation herein provided commence to run until the passage of this act, so that no party shall, by virtue of this act, be debarred of his remedy by suit or prosecution until two years from and after the passage of this act." (Act March 3, 1863, 12 Stat. at L. 757, § 7.)

Whenever, during the existence of the present rebellion, any action, civil or criminal, shall accrue against any person who, by reason of resistance to the execution of the laws of the United States, or the interruption of the ordinary course of judicial proceedings, cannot be served with process for the commencement of such action or the arrest of such person, or whenever, after such action, civil or criminal, shall have accrued, such person cannot, by reason of such resistance of the laws or such interruption of judicial proceedings, be arrested or served with process for the commencement of the action, the time during which such person shall so be beyond the reach of legal process shall not be deemed or taken as any part of the time limited by law for the commencement of such action. (Act June 11, 1864, 13 Stat. at L. 123.)

All suits on Marshals' bonds, if the right of action has already accrued, shall be commenced and prosecuted within three years after the passage of this act, and not afterwards. And all such suits, in case the right of action shall accrue hereafter, shall be commenced and prosecuted within six years after the said right of action shall have accrued, and not afterwards; saving, nevertheless, the rights of infants, *feme coverts* and persons *non compos mentis*, so that they sue within three years after their disabilities are removed. (Act April 10, 1806, 2 Stat. at L. 374, § 4.)

"That the time fixed for the limitation of suits against the sureties of postmasters, by the third section of the act of Congress, entitled, 'An act to reduce into one the several acts establishing and regulating the Post-office Department,' approved March third, one thousand eight hundred and twenty-five, shall not be considered as running in any State, or part thereof, the inhabitants whereof have been by proclamation of the President declared in a state of insurrection, during the time the insurrection shall continue." (Act July 11, 1862, 12 Stat. at L. 530, § 1.)

The time fixed for the limitation of suits against the sureties of postmasters, by the third section of the act of Congress, approved March 3, 1825, above referred to, is repealed by section 16 of the act of July 27, 1868 (2 Pamphlet Laws, 1867–8, 197); and in and by which it is *provided*, that nothing therein contained shall repeal any of the provisions of the act approved July 11, 1862 (12 Stat. at L. 530), entitled, "An act in relation to the Post-office Department."

If on the final settlement of the account of any postmaster it shall appear that such postmaster is indebted to the United States, and suit shall not be instituted within three years after the close of such account, then, and in that case, the sureties on the bond of such postmaster shall not be liable to the United States. (Act July 27, 1868, 2 Pamphlet Laws, 1867–8, 197, § 17.)

Proceedings for the punishment of certain frauds committed by persons in the military or naval service, or by civilians—in presenting fictitious claims against the United States or any department or officer thereof, and making false vouchers, etc., etc.—are to be "commenced within six years from the doing or committing of the act, and not afterwards." (Act March 3, 1863, 12 Stat. at L. 698, § 7.)

SECTION XVII.

NAME.

The law knows of but one Christian name, and the omission or insertion of the middle name, or of the initial letter of that name, is not material. (*Games* v. *Stiles*, 14 Pet. 322.)

Affix "Jr." not an essential part of a name. (*Clark* v. *Gilbert*, Burn. (Wis.) 207.)

SECTION XVIII.

OATHS.

In all cases in which, *under the laws of the United States, oaths or affirmations or acknowledgments* may *now* be taken or made before any *justice or justices of the peace of any State or Territory*, such oaths, affirmations or acknowledgments may be hereafter also taken or made by or before any notary public duly appointed in any State or Territory; and when certified under the hand and official seal of such notary, shall have the same force and effect as if taken or made by or before such justice or justices of the peace: * * *Provided always*, that on any trial for either of these offenses [perjury or subornation of perjury], the seal and signature of the notary shall not be deemed sufficient in themselves to establish the official character of such notary, but the same shall be shown by

GENERAL INFORMATION. 69

other and proper evidence. (Act Sept. 16, 1850, 9 Stat. at L. 458, § 1.)

That *all the powers and authority conferred in and by the preceding section of this act upon notaries public* be and the same are hereby vested in, and may be exercised by, any Commissioner appointed, or hereafter to be appointed, by any Circuit Court of the United States, under any act of Congress authorizing the appointment of Commissioners to take bail, affidavits or depositions, in causes pending in the courts of the United States. (Id. § 2.)

By a resolution passed on the tenth day of April, A. D. 1869, Congress resolved, "That any officer or clerk of any of the executive departments of the government, who shall be lawfully detailed to investigate frauds, or attempts to defraud, on the government, or any irregularity or misconduct of any officer or agent of the United States, shall have power to administer oaths to affidavits taken in the course of any such investigation." (See 1 Pamphlet Laws, 1869, p. 55, § 2.)

See "Affidavits and Depositions."

SECTION XIX.

PARDON.

The President alone has power to grant reprieves and pardons for offenses against the United States, except in cases of impeachment. (U. S. Const. art. II, § 2.)

In order to obtain the pardon of a person under sentence of imprisonment, a petition for that purpose, accompanied by any other additional papers or affidavits as may be deemed necessary, should be forwarded to the President. The petition should, among other things, set forth the nature of the crime of which the prisoner has been convicted; at what term of the court he was convicted; for what period of time he was sentenced; and to what prison or penitentiary. The petition is usually referred by the President to the Attorney-General, by whom it is forwarded to the Attorney of the United States for the District wherein the prisoner was convicted, for a report of the facts in the case, with his opinion thereon. On receiving the report of the District Attorney, the Attorney-General submits the same to the President, by whom (if he so decides) a warrant of pardon is issued to the Marshal of the United States for the District wherein the prisoner is confined, — who communicates the same to the keeper of the prison.

If the prisoner serves the full term of his sentence, without being pardoned, he is, of course, divested of his citizenship. He may, however, be restored to the full rights of a citizen on petition to the President for that purpose, and showing by proper proof that he is worthy of being so restored.

"That (to remove doubts as to the true meaning of former laws), hereafter, whenever by the judgment of any court or judicial officer of the United States, in any criminal proceeding, any person shall be sentenced, or shall have been sentenced heretofore, to two kinds of punishment, the one pecuniary and the other corporal, the President shall have full discretionary power to pardon or remit, in whole or in part,

GENERAL INFORMATION. 71

either one of the two kinds, without in any manner impairing the legal validity of the other kind, or of any portion of either kind, not pardoned or remitted." (Act. Feb. 20, 1863, 12 Stat. at L. 656, § 1.)

SECTION XX.

POWERS, DUTIES AND LIABILITIES OF MARSHALS.

The Deputy of the Marshal is a sworn officer, known to the law, and he may return, according to the general practice, as Deputy, the process served by him. (*Spafford* v. *Goodell*, 3 McL. 97.)

The Deputy Marshal is an officer of the District Court, amenable to its jurisdiction for malfeasance in office; and this jurisdiction may be exercised by summary order or attachment for contempt. (*Bark "Laurens,"* 1 Abb. Adm. 508.)

A Deputy of a Marshal of the United States is an *officer* of the United States, authorized to serve process, within the meaning of section 22, act of Congress, approved April 30, 1790 (1 Stat. at L. 117), which imposes a penalty on any person or persons who shall "knowingly and willfully obstruct, resist or oppose any *officer* of the United States, in serving or attempting to serve or execute any mesne process, or warrant, or any rule or order of any of the courts of the United States, or any other legal or judicial writ or process whatsoever." (*U. S.* v. *Tinklepaugh*, 3 Blatch. C. C. 426.)

"The Marshals of the several Districts of the United States, and their Deputies, shall have the same powers in executing the laws of the United States as Sheriffs and their deputies in the several States have by law, in executing the laws of the respective States." (Act July 29, 1861, 12 Stat. at L. 282, § 7.)

A Marshal of the United States, when opposed in the execution of his duty by unlawful combinations, has authority to summon the entire able-bodied force of his precinct as a *posse comitatus*. (6 Op. Atty.-Gen. 466.)

This authority comprehends not only bystanders and other citizens generally, but any and all organized armed forces, whether militia of the State, or officers, soldiers, sailors and marines of the United States. (Id.)

If a debtor committed to jail under process from the courts of the United States escape, the Marshal is not liable. (*Randolph* v. *Donaldson*, 9 Cranch, 85.)

The act of Congress has limited the responsibility of the Marshal to his own acts and the acts of his Deputies. The keeper of a State jail is neither in fact nor in law the Deputy of the Marshal. He is not appointed by nor removable at the will of the Marshal. When a prisoner is regularly committed to a State jail by the Marshal, he is no longer in the custody of the Marshal nor controllable by him. (Ibid.)

Where a Deputy Marshal receives money on a judgment, after he has returned the execution, he may be attached on a neglect to pay over the amount in pursuance of the order of the court.

The Marshal is responsible for the acts of his Deputy done in the line of his duty.

But when the Deputy does not so act, the Marshal is not responsible.

The Deputy is an officer of the Circuit Court, and may be held responsible as such. (*Bagley* v. *Yates & Prentiss*, 3 McL. 465.)

The service of a summons by a Deputy Marshal, the day after the new Marshal has filed his bond and taken the oath, the process having before been in the hands of the Deputy, is good. (*Stewart* v. *Hamilton*, 4 McL. 534.)

By act of Congress, approved June 21, 1860 (12 Stat. at L. 69, § 1), it is provided that "whenever any Marshal, Deputy Marshal or other ministerial officer, shall have in his custody any prisoner by virtue of process issued under the laws of the United States by any court, Judge or Commissioner, and such Marshal, Deputy Marshal or other ministerial officer, shall voluntarily suffer such prisoner to escape, the officer so offending shall be deemed guilty of a misdemeanor, and, upon conviction thereof in any District or Circuit Court of the United States, shall be fined or imprisoned, or both, according to the discretion of the court in which such conviction shall take place, having respect to the nature of the crime with which the escaped prisoner shall have been charged, in a sum not exceeding two thousand dollars, and for a term not exceeding two years. This act shall be taken and construed to apply not only to cases in which the prisoner who escaped was charged or found guilty of an offense against the laws of the United States, but also to cases in which a prisoner may be in custody, charged with offenses against any foreign government with whom the United States have treaties of extradition."

The Marshal, in his official capacity, has no authority to do any act that shall expressly or impliedly bind any one by warranty. If he steps aside from his official duty, and does what the law has given him no authority to do, he may make himself personally responsible, and the injured party must look to him for redress. The same principle is applicable to any representations of his agent the auctioneer. (*The Monte Allegre*, 9 Wheat. 616.)

The removal of a United States Marshal may be either express, by notice of an order of removal, or implied, by the appointment of another person to the same office. But, in either case, the removal is not completely effected until notice is actually received by the officer removed. His acts, done before such notice, are valid. (*Bowerbank* v. *Morris*, Wall. C. Ct. 118.)

"In case of the death of any Marshal, his Deputy or Deputies shall continue in office, unless otherwise specially removed; and shall execute [all writs and precepts] in the name of the deceased, until another Marshal shall be appointed and sworn: And the defaults or misfeasances in office of such Deputy or Deputies in the mean time, as well as before, shall be adjudged a breach of the condition of the bond given, * * by the Marshal who appointed them; and the executor or administrator of the deceased Marshal shall have like remedy for the defaults and misfeasances in office of such Deputy or Deputies during such interval, as they would be entitled to if the Marshal had continued in life and the exercise of his said office, until his successor was appointed, and sworn or affirmed:

GENERAL INFORMATION. 75

And every Marshal or his Deputy when removed from office, or when the term for which the Marshal is appointed shall expire, shall have power, notwithstanding, to execute all such precepts as may be in their hands respectively at the time of such removal or expiration of office; and the Marshal shall be held answerable for the delivery to his successor of all prisoners which may be in his custody at the time of his removal, or when the term for which he is appointed shall expire, and for that purpose may retain such prisoners in his custody until his successor shall be appointed and qualified as the law directs." (Act Sept. 24, 1789, 1 Stat. at L. 87, § 28.)

A Marshal appointed while such District covered the entire State, continued in office, after the State was divided, as Marshal of both Districts, and his bail continued liable for his acts. (5 Op. Atty.-Gen. 96.)

Where a writ of *capias ad respondendum* comes to the hands of a Deputy Marshal, who arrests the debtor, and the debtor thereupon pays to the Deputy the amount of the debt for which he was sued, and the officer discharges the debtor from custody, and returns the writ " debt and costs satisfied," this is not an official act which binds his principal. The Deputy Marshal is a mere ministerial officer, and he has no right to adjust the debt, and make himself responsible to the plaintiff. He is bound to pursue the mandate of the writ, and that requires him to arrest the debtor and take bail. (*U. S.* v. *Moore*, 2 Brock. Marsh. 317.)

If the plaintiff has received the debt and costs, the Marshal cannot detain the defendant upon a *ca. sa.* for the poundage. (*Causin* v. *Chubb*, 1 Cranch C. Ct. 267.)

When a writ of habeas corpus is served on a Marshal or other person having a prisoner in custody under the authority of the United States, it is his duty, by a proper return, to make known to the State Judge or court the authority by which he holds such prisoner. But it is his duty, at the same time, not to obey the State process, but to execute that of the United States. (*Ableman* v. *Booth*, 21 How. 506.)

As to the liability of an officer, all writs and process of the courts may be divided into two classes:

1. Those which point out specifically the property or thing to be seized.

2. Those which command the officer to make or levy certain sums of money, out of property of a party named.

In the first class the officer has no discretion, but must do precisely what he is commanded. Therefore, if the court had jurisdiction to issue the writ, it is a protection to the officer in all courts. But in the second class the officer must determine for himself whether the property which he proposes to seize under the process is legally liable to be so taken, and the court can afford him no protection against the consequences of an erroneous exercise of his judgment in that determination. He is liable to suit for injuries growing out of such mistakes, in any court of competent jurisdiction. (*Buck* v. *Colbath*, 3 Wall. 334.)

SECTION XXI.

PRISONERS.

No writ shall be necessary to bring into court any prisoner or person in custody, or for remanding him from the court into custody; but the same shall be done on the order of the court or District Attorney, for which no fee shall be charged by the Clerk or Marshal. (Act Feb. 26, 1853, 10 Stat. at L. 169, § 3.)

When a prisoner is regularly committed to a State jail by the Marshal, he is no longer in the custody of the Marshal, nor controllable by him. The Marshal has no authority to command or direct the keeper in respect to the nature of the imprisonment. (*Randolph* v. *Donaldson*, 9 Cranch, 85.)

"Whenever any criminal, convicted of any offense against the United States, shall be imprisoned, in pursuance of such conviction and of the sentence thereupon, in the prison or penitentiary of any State or Territory, such criminal shall, in all respects, be subject to the same discipline and treatment as convicts sentenced by the courts of the State or Territory in which such prison or penitentiary is situated; and while so confined therein, shall also be exclusively under the control of the officers having charge of the same, under the laws of the said State or Territory." (Act June 30, 1834, 4 Stat. at L. 739.)

"In every case where any person convicted of any offense against the United States shall be sentenced to imprisonment for a period longer than one year, it shall be lawful for the court by which the sentence is passed, to order the same to be executed in any State prison or penitentiary within the District or State where such court is held, the use of which prison or penitentiary is allowed by the Legislature of such State for such purposes; and the expenses attendant upon the execution of such sentence shall be paid by the United States." (Act March 3, 1865, 13 Stat. at L. 500, § 3.)

"Juvenile offenders against the laws of the United States, being under the age of sixteen years, and who may hereafter be convicted of crime by any court of the United States, the punishment whereof shall be imprisonment, shall be confined, during the term of sentence, in some house of refuge, to be designated by the Secretary of the Interior, and shall be transported and delivered to the warden or keeper of such house of refuge by the Marshal of the District where such shall have occurred." (Act March 3, 1865, 13 Stat. at L. 538, § 1.)

Whenever a prisoner is committed to a Sheriff or jailor by virtue of a writ, warrant or mittimus, a copy thereof shall be delivered to the Sheriff or jailor, as his authority to hold the prisoner, and the original writ, warrant or mittimus shall be returned to the proper court or officer, with the officer's return thereon. (Act Feb. 26, 1853, 10 Stat. at L. 163.)

Convicts under the laws of the United States, confined in any State prison or penitentiary in execution of the judgment or sentence upon such conviction, who so conduct themselves that no charge for misconduct shall be sustained against them, shall have a deduction of one month in each year made from the term of their sentence, and shall be entitled to their discharge so much the sooner, upon the certificate of the warden or keeper of such prison or penitentiary, with the approval of the Secretary of the Interior. (Act March 2, 1867, 14 Stat. at L. 424.)

SECTION XXII.

PROCESS.

Process returnable forthwith, should be executed within twenty-four hours.

Process may be served in any part of the District in which it is issued, and the service may be made either by the Marshal, by his general Deputy, or by a special Deputy or Bailiff constituted for that purpose by the Marshal.

Whenever two or more charges are or shall be made, or two or more indictments shall be found, against a person, only one writ or warrant shall be necessary to arrest and commit him for trial; and it shall be sufficient to state in the writ the name or general character of the offenses, or to refer to them in very general terms. Only one writ or warrant shall be necessary to remove a prisoner from one District to another; a copy of which may be delivered to the Sheriff or jailor from whose custody the prisoner may be taken, and another copy thereof to the Sheriff or jailor to whose custody he may be committed, and the original writ, with the Marshal's return thereon, shall be returned to the clerk of the District to which he may be removed. (Act Feb. 26, 1853, 10 Stat. at L. 162.)

In all causes wherein the Marshal or his Deputy shall be a party, the writs and precepts therein shall be directed to such disinterested person as the court, or any justice or judge thereof, may appoint; and the person so appointed is hereby authorized to execute and return the same. (Act Sept. 24, 1789, 1 Stat. at L. 87, § 28.)

The courts of the United States, and those of a State, have concurrent jurisdiction in many cases; and where persons or property are liable to seizure or arrest by the process of both, that which first attached has the preference.

Where a person is properly in custody under State authority, the Circuit Court has no authority to take the accused by *habeas corpus* from such custody. Nor has a State court authority to remove a defendant from the custody of a court of the United States. (*U. S.* v. *Rector*, 5 McLean, 174; 6 Op. Atty.-Gen. 713.)

In equity, when husband and wife are co-defendants, service upon the husband alone is good service of a writ of subpœna. (*Robinson* v. *Cathcart*, 2 Cranch C. C. 590.)

GENERAL INFORMATION. 81

SECTION XXIII.

SEIZURE CASES.

These are either of *Admiralty* or *Common Law* jurisdiction. The first embrace all cases of seizure *on water*, and are commenced by the filing of a *Libel*, when the suit is between private parties, and of a *Libel of Information*, when proceedings are instituted on the part of the Government. The latter include all seizures of property *on land*, generally by officers of the revenue, and are commenced by the filing of an *Information*.

Actions in Admiralty are either *in rem* (against the thing), or *in personam* (against the person). The party bringing the suit is called the *Libellant*. The person claiming the property is called the *Claimant*; and he against whom an action is brought is called the *Respondent*.

While in actions at Common Law, the person who institutes the action is called the *Plaintiff*; the person claiming the property is called the *Claimant*; and he against whom an action is brought is called the *Defendant*.

The officers of court by whom proceedings in admiralty are conducted in behalf of suitors, are called *Proctors* and *Advocates*; which terms are equivalent to *Attorneys* and *Counselors* at Common Law, and to *Solicitors* and *Counselors* in *Equity*.

On making a *seizure*, the Marshal is required to give notice thereof by publication "in some news-

11

paper published near the place of seizure, and also by posting up the same in the most public manner, for the space of fourteen days, at or near the place of trial; for which advertisement a sum not exceeding ten dollars shall be paid." (Act March 2, 1799, 1 Stat. at L. 695, § 89.)

He is also required to give at least fifteen days' notice (except in case of perishable goods) of the time and place of *sale* of property, by publication "in one or more of the public newspapers of the place where such sale shall be; or, if no paper is published in such place, in one or more of the papers published in the nearest place thereto; for which advertising a sum not exceeding five dollars shall be paid." (Act March 2, 1799, 1 Stat. at L. 696, § 90.)

Under the act of Congress, of March 2, 1799 (1 Stat. at L. 696, § 90), the notices of sale in cases of condemnation under the act must be published every day for fifteen days in the newspapers directed by the act. (*The Hornet*, 1 Abb. Adm. 57.)

In seizure cases the Deputy Marshal is very often required to place a person in charge of the property seized. But before doing so, he should agree on the amount to be paid for such service, which must not exceed the rate and sum of two dollars and fifty cents per day. On discharging such person, the Deputy should pay him the amount due and take duplicate vouchers therefor — one of which he should transmit to the Marshal, and the other retain. If the amount so paid exceeds fifty cents per day, the bills should be sworn to. (See forms 9 and 19.)

"Whenever two or more things belonging to the same person or persons are or shall be seized for an alleged violation of the revenue laws, the whole shall be included in one suit; and if not so included, and separate actions are prosecuted, the court may consolidate them." (Act Feb. 26, 1853, 10 Stat. at L. 162.)

At the March Term, 1869, of the United States District Court for the Northern District of New York, held at Utica, an order was made in reference to the publication of Marshal's notices, a copy of which will be found in Appendix (B).

On completing a sale of property, the Deputy should obtain and forward to the Marshal proper vouchers for all disbursements made, together with the warrant under which the sale was had, with his proper return indorsed thereon, and also the amount realized from such sale.

SECTION XXIV.

SUBPŒNAS AND WITNESSES.

Subpœnas for witnesses who may be required to attend a court of the United States, in any District thereof, may run into any other District: *Provided*, that in *civil* causes, the witnesses living out of the District in which the court is holden, do not live at a greater distance than one hundred miles from the place of holding the same. (Act March 2, 1793, 1 Stat. at L. 335, § 6.)

Whenever any indictment shall be pending in any court of the United States, and any defendant thereto shall make an affidavit setting forth that there are witnesses whose evidence is material to his defense, and that he cannot safely go to trial without them, what he expects to prove by each of them, that they are in the District in which the court is held, or within one hundred miles of the place of trial, and that he is not possessed of sufficient means, and is actually unable to pay the fees of such witnesses, the court in term, or any judge thereof in vacation, may, if it appear proper to do so, order that such witnesses be subpœnaed, if found within the limits aforesaid; and in such case the costs incurred by such process and the fees of such witnesses shall be paid in the same manner that similar costs and fees are paid in case of witnesses subpœnaed in behalf of the United States. (Act Aug. 8, 1846, 9 Stat. at L. 74 § 11.)

In the courts of the United States there shall be no exclusion of any witness on account of color, nor in civil actions because he is a party to, or interested in, the issue tried. (Act July 2, 1864, 13 Stat. at L. 351, § 3.)

No officer of the United States, who is in attendance upon any court of the United States, in the discharge of the duties of said office, shall receive any pay or compensation for his attendance as a witness on behalf of the government, at the same time that he receives compensation as such officer. (Act July 21, 1852, 10 Stat. at L. 22, § 1.)

" In no case shall the fees of more than four witnesses be taxed against the United States in the examination of criminal cases before the Commissioners of the United States Circuit Courts, unless their materiality and importance shall first be approved and certified to by the United States District

GENERAL INFORMATION. 85

Attorney for the District in which the examination shall take place, subject to revision, as in other cases." (Act Aug. 16, 1856, 11 Stat. at L. 49, § 3.)

No officer of the United States courts, including the bailiffs, guards, or deputies of the United States Marshals, whether in the States, Territories, or District of Columbia, shall be entitled to witness fees, either before a court or commissioners where he is officiating. (Id. § 8.)

In all hearings before any justice or judge of the United States, or any Commissioner of the Circuit Court, where the crime or offense is charged to have been committed on the high seas or elsewhere within the admiralty and maritime jurisdiction of the United States, it is lawful for such justice, judge or commissioner, in his discretion, to require a recognizance of any witness produced in behalf of the accused, with such surety or sureties as he may judge necessary, as well as in behalf of the United States, for their appearing and giving testimony, at the trial of the cause, whose testimony, in his opinion, is important for the purposes of justice at the trial of the cause, and is in danger of being otherwise lost; and such witnesses shall be entitled to receive from the United States the usual compensation allowed to government witnesses for their detention and attendance, if they shall appear and be ready to give testimony at the trial. (Act Aug. 23, 1842, 5 Stat. at L. 517, § 2.)

On the application of any attorney of the United States for any District, and upon satisfactory proof of the materiality of the testimony of any person who shall be a competent witness, and whose testimony shall, in the opinion of any judge of the United States, be necessary upon the trial of any criminal cause or proceeding in which the United States shall be a party or interested, any such Judge may compel such person, so required or deemed by him necessary as a witness, to give recognizance, with or without sureties, in his discretion, to appear on the trial of said cause or proceeding and give his testimony therein; and for that purpose, the said Judge may issue a warrant against such person, under his hand, with or without seal, directed to the Marshal or other officer authorized to execute civil or criminal process in behalf of the United States, to arrest such person and carry him before such Judge. And in case the person so arrested shall neglect or refuse to give said recognizance in the manner required by said Judge, the said Judge may issue a warrant of commitment against such person, which shall be delivered to said officer, whose duty it shall be to convey such person to the prison mentioned in said mittimus. And the said person shall remain in confinement until he shall be removed to the court for the purpose of giving his testimony, or until he shall have given the recognizance required by said Judge. (Act Aug. 8, 1846, 9 Stat. at L. 73, § 7.)

"Witnesses who are required to attend any term of the court on the part of the United States, shall be subpœnaed to attend to testify generally on their behalf, and not depart the court without leave of the court or District Attorney, under which it shall be their duty to appear before the Grand Jury or Petit Jury, or both, as they shall be required by the court or District Attorney." (Act February 26, 1853, 10 Stat. at L. 169, § 3.)

When a witness is detained in prison for want of security for his appearance, he shall be entitled to a compensation of one dollar per day over and above his subsistence. (Id. p. 167.)

When a Clerk, or other officer of the United States, shall be sent away from his place of business as a witness for the Government, either with or without papers or books, his salary shall continue; his necessary expenses, stated in items and sworn to, in going, returning, and attendance on the court, shall be audited and paid, but no mileage nor other compensation shall in any case be allowed. (Id.)

There shall be paid to such seamen or other person, as has been or shall be sent to the United States, from any foreign port, station, sea, or ocean, by any United States Minister, *Chargé d' Affaires*, Consul, Commander, or Captain, to give testimony in any criminal case, which has been or may be depending in any court of the United States, such compensation as the court which had or shall have cognizance of the crime, shall adjudge to be right and proper, not to exceed one dollar for each day the said seaman or person has been or shall be necessarily on the voyage, and arriving at the place of examination or trial, exclusive of sustenance or transportation; the court to take into consideration, in fixing said compensation, the condition of said seaman or witness; whether his voyage has been broken up, to his injury, by his being sent to the United States, or not.

If said seaman or person has been or shall be transported in an armed vessel of the United States, no charge for sustenance or transportation shall be made; if in any other vessel, the court may adjudge what compensation shall be paid to the captain of said vessel, and the same shall be paid accordingly: *Provided,* that in no case shall transportation and subsistence be allowed at a rate exceeding fifty cents per diem. (Id.)

By section 2, act March 2, 1855 (10 Stat. at L. 630), Commissioners of the Circuit Court have power to compel witnesses to appear and depose to Letters Rogatory addressed from any court of a foreign government.

PART II.

FORMS FOR RETURNS IN INFORMATION SUITS.

PART II.

FORMS FOR RETURNS IN INFORMATION SUITS.

No. 1.

RETURN TO ATTACHMENT.

Property seized and in custody.

In obedience to the within writ, I did, on the   day of   , A. D. 18 , at   , in my District, seize and attach the within mentioned property [if the whole of the property is not attached, here say, "except   "], and now have the same in my custody and possession at   aforesaid; and I have duly cited all persons to appear and assert their claims as I am within commanded.

Dated   .

, *U. S. Marshal*,

by   , *Deputy*.

Service, $.

Travel,   miles, at   c. per mile, $.

No. 2.

Return to Attachment.

Property seized and released by order of Court.

In obedience to the within writ, I did, on the   day of   , A. D. 18 , at   , in my District, seize and attach the within mentioned property [if the whole of the property is not attached, here say, " except   "], and I have duly cited all persons to appear and assert their claims, as I am within commanded. Subsequently, having received the annexed certified copy of an order of this court, directing the release of said property, I did thereupon immediately release the same.

Dated   .

, *U. S. Marshal,*

by   , *Deputy.*

Service, $.
Travel,   miles, at   c. per mile, $.
Discharging property, $.

No. 3.

Return to Attachment.

Property not found.

I certify that, after diligent search, I am unable to find the within described property, or any part thereof, within my District.

Dated   .

, *U. S. Marshal,*

by   , *Deputy.*

INFORMATION SUITS. 93

No. 4.

MARSHAL'S NOTICE OF SEIZURE.

No. . [*Internal*] *Revenue Seizure — Marshal's Notice.*

UNITED STATES OF AMERICA, }
DISTRICT OF   . } *ss.*

Whereas [an information, or a libel of information], hath been filed in the District Court of the United States of America, for the District of   , on the   day of   , in the year of our Lord, one thousand eight hundred and   , by   , Esquire, United States Attorney, in behalf of the United States of America, against [here specify the property proceeded against], stating that the same were, on the   day of   , by   , Esquire, Collector of   for the   District of   , seized as forfeited to the use of the said United States; and further stating and alleging that the said forfeiture was incurred by reason of [here state the cause of the seizure], and for other reasons, as will more fully appear by reference to the said [information, or libel of information] on file with the Clerk of said court, at   , and praying the usual process and monition of the said court, that all persons interested in the said property above mentioned and described, etc., etc., may be cited to answer the premises, and all due proceedings being had, that the same may be condemned and sold, and the proceeds thereof be distributed according to law: *Therefore*, in pursuance of the said monition, under the seal of the said court, to me directed and delivered, I do hereby give notice unto all persons generally, having or pretending to have any right, title or interest therein, to appear before the aforesaid court, in the city of   , on the   day of   next, if it be a court day, or else on the next court day thereafter, at ten o'clock in the forenoon, then and there to answer the said [information, or libel of information], and to make their allegations in that behalf.

Dated at   , the   day of   , in the year of our Lord one thousand eight hundred and   .

                                              , *U. S. Marshal,*

                  by   , *Deputy.*

, *U. S. Attorney.*

No. 5.

RETURN TO WARRANT OF MONITION, ISSUED WHERE THE PROPERTY HAS BEEN RELEASED ON BOND BY AN INTERNAL REVENUE OFFICER.

In obedience to the within writ, I have summoned and given notice to the several persons therein named, as follows [here insert the mode of service, which should be made in either of the following ways]:

1. To [John Doe], on the   day of   , 18   , at   , in my District, by ["personally showing him the said writ, and leaving with him a copy thereof"].

2. To [Richard Roe], on the   day of   , 18   , at   , in my District, by ["leaving a copy of said writ at the usual place of abode of said [Roe] with a person of suitable age and discretion"].

INFORMATION SUITS. 95

3. To [John Smith], on the   day of   , 18 ,
at   , in my District, by ["publishing a copy of
said writ three times in each of the following named newspapers designated for the publication of notices in bankruptcy, viz. (here insert the names of the newspapers)"]:

Dated   ·   .

, *U. S. Marshal,*

by   , *Deputy.*

Service, $.

Travel,   miles, at   c. per mile, $.

———

No. 6.

Return to Warrant of Sale.

Property sold.

In obedience to the within warrant of sale [or, warrant of sale *pendente lite*], I did, on the   day of   ,
18 , at   , in my District, sell at public auction, after due notice, as required by law, the within mentioned property, for the sum of   dollars ($), that being the highest sum bid therefor.

Dated

, *U. S. Marshal,*

by   , *Deputy.*

No. 7.

RETURN TO WARRANT OF SALE.

Property not sold.

I certify that I have been unable to sell the within mentioned property, and the same now remains on hand for want of bidders [or for any other cause arising]; therefore I cannot have the moneys at the day and place within mentioned, as I am within commanded.

Dated   .

                                                    , *U. S. Marshal.*
                        by   , *Deputy.*

No. 8.

MARSHAL'S NOTICE OF SALE.

[*Internal*] *Revenue Sale*   , *No.*   .

By virtue of a warrant of sale [or, warrant of sale *pendente lite*], issued out of the District Court of the United States of America for the District of   , and to me directed and delivered: I shall sell at public auction, to the highest bidder, for cash, on [Tuesday] the day of   , 18 , at [here insert the place of sale], in the city of   , the following described property, to wit:

[Here describe the property.]

[If the property has been condemned, then add, "condemned at the suit of the United States."]

Dated   ,   .

                                                    , *U. S. Marshal,*
                        by   , *Deputy.*

INFORMATION SUITS. 97

Notice of Postponement of Sale.

The above sale is postponed until [Tuesday] the day of   , 18 , at the same time and place.

Dated   ,   .

                                , *U. S. Marshal*,

            by   , *Deputy.*

———

No. 9.

BILL AND AFFIDAVIT OF STOREKEEPER.

                   ,
U. S. Marshal, District of   ,

            To   , *Dr.:*

For services as storekeeper in charge of the property seized from   , for the period from   , 18 , to   , 18 , both days inclusive, being   days, at $ per day,... $.

Received   , 18 , from   , U. S. Marshal for the District of   , per   , Deputy,   dollars, in full payment of the foregoing bill.

UNITED STATES OF AMERICA, } *ss:*
  DISTRICT OF   . }

              , being duly sworn, says: that the service charged in the foregoing bill has been actually rendered as therein stated; that he has been paid therefor the sum of   dollars; that the same was received for said service only, and wholly for his own use and benefit, and not for the benefit of any officer of the court; and further, that there is no understanding, express or implied, that the whole or any part of said sum shall be paid, or in any way disposed of, or allowed, to the Marshal or his Deputy, or for his or their benefit.

Subscribed and sworn to, this
　day of　　　　　　, 18　, before me.

The bill should be folded, and indorsed with the number and title of the suit and the title of the court, and also with the following, viz.:

" Bill of　　　　　　, Storekeeper, $　　."

No. 10.

MARSHAL'S BILL.

DISTRICT COURT OF THE UNITED STATES
　FOR THE　　　　　　DISTRICT OF　　　　　:

The United States
　　vs.　　　　　} No　.
Six casks of whisky.

Serving mesne process at　　　, ret. at　　.. $2 00
Travel to return the same,　　miles at six cents.
Proclamation ....　　30
Expenses of custody actually paid................
Oath and certificate disbursements................　25
Paid printer publishing notice of arrest ....

INFORMATION SUITS. 99

Serving warrant to sell at   , ret. at   .. $2 00
Travel to return the same,   miles at six cents.
Paid printer publishing notice of sale., ...
Poundage on $, amount of sale (see State Law)
Fee for advertising sale (see State Law) 2 00
Percentage on disbursements ....
Service and travel upon subpœna ret. Augt. Tr. 1869

Taxed at $, this   day }
   of   , 18 .   }
                                     , *Clerk.*

  UNITED STATES OF AMERICA,   } *ss:*
NORTHERN DISTRICT OF NEW YORK, }

                , Marshal of the said District, being duly sworn deposes and says, that the services charged in the foregoing bill have been actually and necessarily performed as therein stated, and that the expenses mentioned in said bill, have been actually and necessarily incurred as therein set forth.

Subscribed and sworn before me, }
   this   day of   , 18 . }

                        ,
              United States Commissioner.

PART III.

FORMS FOR RETURNS IN ADMIRALTY CASES.

PART III.

FORMS FOR RETURNS IN ADMIRALTY CASES.

No. 11.

RETURN TO WARRANT OF ARREST AND MONITION.

Vessel seized and in custody.

In obedience to the within writ, I did, on the   day of   , 18 , at   , in my District, arrest the within mentioned [schooner]   , her tackle, apparel and furniture, and now have the same in my custody at   aforesaid; and I have duly cited all persons to appear, as I am within commanded.

Dated   .

, *U. S. Marshal,*

by   , *Deputy.*

Service, $.

Travel,   miles, at   c. per mile, $.

No. 12.

RETURN TO WARRANT OF ARREST AND MONITION.

Vessel seized and released on bond.

In obedience to the within writ, I did, on the   day of   , 18 , at   , in my District, arrest the within mentioned [schooner]   , her tackle, apparel and furniture; and I have duly cited all persons to appear and assert their claims, as I am within commanded. Subsequently, having received a bond in the sum of $, duly approved by   , and conditioned to abide and answer the decree of the court in this cause, I immediately released the said [schooner], and return the said bond herewith.

Dated   .

            , *U. S. Marshal*,

        by   , *Deputy.*

Service, $.

Travel,   miles, at   c. per mile, $.

Bond, $.

No. 13.

RETURN TO WARRANT OF ARREST AND MONITION.

Vessel not seized.

I certify, that after diligent search, I am unable to find the within mentioned [schooner]   , her tackle, apparel and furniture, within my District.

Dated   .

            , *U. S. Marshal*,

        by   , *Deputy.*

No. 14.

MARSHAL'S NOTICE — ADMIRALTY SEIZURE.

The [*Schooner*]

UNITED STATES OF AMERICA, }
DISTRICT OF   . }

Whereas, a libel hath been filed in the District Court of the United States of America for the District of   , on the   day of   , in the year of our Lord one thousand eight hundred and   , by   , Esq., Proctor, in behalf of [here insert the name of libellant and the substance of the libel], and praying the usual process and monition of the court, that all persons interested in the said vessel, her tackle, apparel and furniture, may be cited to answer the premises, and all due proceedings being had, that the same may be decreed to be sold, and the proceeds thereof be distributed according to law: *Therefore*, in pursuance of the said monition under the seal of said court, to me directed and delivered, I do hereby give notice generally, unto all persons having or pretending to have any right, title or interest therein, and to   , master of the said   , in special, to appear before the aforesaid court, at the city of   , on the   day of   , if it be a court day, or else on the next court day thereafter, at ten o'clock in the forenoon, then and there to answer the said libel and to make their allegations in that behalf.

[If it is an action for seaman's wages, here add: "And also to answer unto all other persons having claims against the said vessel, for wages earned on board thereof, who may choose to make themselves parties to the libel of the said   , by way of amendment or supplement, without further process or citation."]

Dated at   the   day of   , in the year of our Lord one thousand eight hundred and   .

, *Proctor.*

, *U. S. Marshal.*

, *Deputy.*

No. 15.

RETURN TO MONITION.

I certify that I have monished and cited all persons to appear before the said court at the time and place as I am within commanded.

Dated

, *U. S. Marshal,*

by   , *Deputy.*

Service, $.

Travel,   miles, at   c. per mile, $.

No. 16.

MARSHAL'S NOTICE ON MONITION.

No. .

UNITED STATES OF AMERICA, }
  DISTRICT OF   . }

Whereas, a petition hath been filed in the District Court of the United States of America for the District of   , on the   day of   , in the year of our Lord one thousand eight hundred and   , by   , Esq., Proctor, in behalf of   , of   , in the State of   , against the proceeds of the sale of the

IN ADMIRALTY CASES. 107

[schooner]   , now in the registry of the said court, stating and alleging that [here state the allegations of the petition], and praying the usual process and monition of the said court, that all persons having or pretending to have any right, title or interest therein, may be cited to answer the premises, and all due proceedings being had, that the demand of the petitioner may be decreed to be paid out of the said proceeds: *Therefore*, in pursuance of the said monition, under the seal of the said court, to me directed and delivered, I do hereby give notice generally, unto all persons having or pretending to have any right, title or interest in the said proceeds, to appear before the said court, at the city of   , on the   day of   , if it shall be a court day, otherwise on the next court day thereafter, at ten o'clock in the forenoon, to answer the petition of the said   , and further to do and receive in this behalf as to justice shall appertain.

Dated at   the   day of   , in the year of our Lord one thousand eight hundred and   .

, *Proctor*.

, *U. S. Marshal*,

, *Deputy*.

No. 17.

RETURN TO VENDITIONI EXPONAS.

I certify, that on the   day of   , 18 , at   , in my District, in pursuance of the within process, and after due notice as required by law, I sold the within mentioned [schooner]   , her engines, boats, tackle, apparel and furniture, at public auction, to   , of the city of   , for the sum of   dollars ($), that being the highest bid therefor, and he being the highest bidder; and that I have paid the said sum into the registry of the said court, as I am within commanded.

Dated   .

         , *U. S. Marshal,*

      by   , *Deputy.*

No. 18.

MARSHAL'S NOTICE OF SALE UPON EXECUTION IN ADMIRALTY.

By virtue of a writ of venditioni exponas, issued out of the District Court of the United States for the District of   , at the suit of   , I will expose to sale at public auction, and will sell to the best bidder, for cash, on [Tuesday], the   day of   , 18 , at   o'clock in the forenoon, the [schooner] , her tackle, apparel and furniture, boats and appurtenances, where she now lies, at [here state the place where the vessel is harbored] in the city of   .

Dated   .

         , *U. S. Marshal,*

      by   , *Deputy.*

No. 19.

BILL AND AFFIDAVIT OF SHIPKEEPER.

   , *U. S. Marshal, District of*   ,
      To   , *Dr.*

For services as shipkeeper, in charge of the [schooner "America"], for the period from   , 18 , to , 18 , both days inclusive, being   days, at $ per day, ... $.

IN ADMIRALTY CASES. 109

Received,   ,   , 18 , from
, U. S. Marshal, for the District of   , per
      , Deputy,   dollars, in full payment
of the foregoing bill.

(For affidavit, see Form No. .)

The bill should be folded, and indorsed with the number and title of the suit and the title of the court, and also with the following, viz.:

" Bill of   , Shipkeeper, $."

No. 20.

RETURN TO WARRANT IN PERSONAM.

Defendant arrested and in custody.

I certify, that on the   day of   , 18 ,
at   , in my District, I arrested the within named   , and now have him before this court, as within I am commanded.

Dated   .

                       , *U. S. Marshal*,

           by   , *Deputy*.

Service, $.

Travel,   miles, at   c. per mile, $

No. 21.

RETURN TO WARRANT IN PERSONAM.

Defendant arrested and discharged on bail.

I certify, that on the   day of   , 18   , at   , in my District, I arrested the within named   . Subsequently, having received a bond in the sum of $, conditioned that the said   should abide the decree of the court in this cause, I discharged the said defendant, and return the said bond herewith.

Dated   .

, *U. S. Marshal*,

by   , *Deputy*.

Service, $.

Travel,   miles, at   c. per mile, $.

Discharging defendant, $.

No. 22.

RETURN TO WARRANT IN PERSONAM.

Defendant not found.

I certify, that after diligent search, I am unable to find the within named   in my District, so that I may have him before this court, as within I am commanded.

Dated   .

, *U. S. Marshal*,

by   , *Deputy*.

IN ADMIRALTY CASES. 111

No. 23.

MARSHAL'S BILL.

DISTRICT COURT OF THE UNITED STATES
FOR THE   DISTRICT OF

John Doe

v.

The schooner " Elizabeth,"
her tackle, etc.

} No. .

Serving mesne process at , ret. at ,..	$2 00
Travel to return the same miles, at six cents,..	
Proclamation, ...	30
Expenses of custody actually paid, ...	
Oath and certificate disbursements,...............	25
Paid printer publishing notice of arrest, ...	
Serving warrant to sell at , ret. at ,...	2 00
Travel to return the same miles, at six cents,..	
Paid printer publishing notice of sale, ...	
Poundage on $ amount of sale (see State Law),..	
Fee for advertising sale (see State Law),............	
Percentage on disbursements,....................	
Paid postage, ...	

Taxed at $ this day }
 of   , 18 .

, *Clerk.*

UNITED STATES OF AMERICA, }
NORTHERN DISTRICT OF NEW YORK. } *ss.*

, Marshal of the said District, being duly sworn, deposes and says, that the services charged in the foregoing bill have been actually and necessarily performed as therein stated, and that the expenses mentioned in said bill, have been actually and necessarily incurred as therein set forth.

Subscribed and sworn before me this   day of   , 18 .

, *U. S. Commissioner.*

No. 24.

DEED OF A VESSEL, WITH CERTIFICATE OF ENROLLMENT.

To all to whom these presents shall come, GREETING :

Know ye, that whereas by virtue of a [writ of *venditioni exponas,* or warrant to sell *pendente lite*] issued out of the District Court of the United States of America for the District of   , tested at   , on the   day of   , in the year of our Lord one thousand eight hundred and   , directed and delivered to the undersigned, the Marshal of the United States for the District of   , I, the said Marshal, was commanded that I should cause to be sold, the [brig " Lowell,". her boats, tackle, apparel and furniture] in the manner and form by law required, pursuant to [a decree] or [an order] made by the said court, on the said   day of   , in a certain cause pending therein, wherein   and   are libellants, against the said [brig " Lowell," her boats, tackle, apparel and furniture], which same, at the time of the making of the said [decree] or [order] and issuing the aforesaid writ, were in the custody of the said court, in virtue of the process thereof, issued in pursuance of the libel in the said cause, as by reference to the said writ [decree] or [order], and libel and other proceedings remaining of record in the said court, will more fully appear. And whereas, after the delivery to me of the said writ, and before the return day thereof, I did in obedience to the mandate of the said writ, and in virtue thereof, expose for sale

IN ADMIRALTY CASES. 113

at public auction, the said [brig "Lowell," her boats, tackle, apparel, furniture and appurtenances], at the city of   , in the said District, after having given due notice of the time and place of such sale as by law required, and on such sale did strike off and sell the said [brig "Lowell," her boats, tackle, apparel, furniture and appurtenances,] to   of the city of   , for the sum of   dollars, that being the best bid and he being the best bidder therefor, and which said sale was made on the   day of   , Anno Domini, 18 . And whereas the said   , the purchaser aforesaid, has paid to me, the said Marshal, the said sum so bid by him upon such sale as aforesaid.

Now therefore know ye, that I, the said Marshal, in virtue of the said writ, and of the sale so made in pursuance thereof, and of the statute in such case made and provided, and in consideration of the said sum of money so to me paid by the said   , have granted, bargained, sold, conveyed and delivered, and by these presents do grant, bargain, sell, convey and deliver, unto the said   , the said [brig "Lowell"] with all and singular her [boats, tackle, apparel and furniture] of every name and description whatsoever, as the same are now lying and being at the port of   , in the said District, and [the certificate of whose last enrollment is in the words and figures following, to wit:], or [a copy of whose last certificate of enrollment is hereunto annexed, and making a part of this conveyance]. To have and to hold the said granted and described [brig "Lowell," her boats, tackle, apparel and furniture], and every part thereof, to the sole and only use, benefit and behoof of the said   , his heirs and assigns forever, as fully and absolutely as I, the said Marshal, under and by virtue of the authority aforesaid, might, could or ought to convey the same.

In witness whereof, I have hereunto set my hand and seal this   day of   , in the year of our Lord one thousand eight hundred and   .   [L. S.]

No. 25.

DEED OF A VESSEL, NO ENROLLMENT.

To all to whom these presents shall come, GREETING :

Know ye, that whereas, by virtue of a writ of *venditioni exponas*, issued out of the District Court of the United States of America for the District of   , tested at   , in the said District, the   day of   , in the year of our Lord one thousand eight hundred and   , directed and delivered to the undersigned, the Marshal of the United States for the District of   , I, the said Marshal, was commanded that I should cause to be sold the [schooner " Ida," her boats, tackle, apparel and furniture], in the manner and form by law required, pursuant to a decree made by the said court, on the   day of   , in the year of our Lord one thousand eight hundred and   , in a certain cause pending therein, wherein   is libellant against the said [schooner " Ida," her boats, tackle, apparel and furniture], and which were, at the time of the making of the said decree and issuing the aforesaid writ, in the custody of the said court, by virtue of the process thereof issued in pursuance of the libel in said cause, as by reference to the said writ, decree and libel, and other proceedings remaining of record in the said court, will more fully appear. And whereas, after the delivery to me of the said writ of *venditioni exponas*, and before the return day thereof, I did, in obedience to the mandate of the said writ, and in virtue thereof, expose for sale at public auction, the said [schooner " Ida," her boats, tackle, apparel and furniture], at the city of   , in the said District, after having given due notice of the time and place of such sale, as by law required, and on such sale did strike off and sell the said [schooner " Ida," her boats, tackle, apparel and furniture], to   , of the city of   , for the sum of   dollars, that being the best bid and he being the best bidder therefor, and which said sale was made on the   day of   , A. D. 18 . And whereas, the said   , the purchaser aforesaid, has paid to me, the said Marshal, the said sum so bid by him upon such sale as aforesaid;

Now, therefore, know ye, that I, the said Marshal, in virtue of the said writ of *venditioni exponas*, and of the sale so made in pursuance thereof, and of the statute in such case made and provided, and in consideration of the said sum of money so to me paid by the said   , have granted, bargained, sold, conveyed and delivered, and by these presents do grant, bargain, sell, convey and deliver, unto the said   , the said [schooner "Ida"], together with all and singular her [boats, tackle, apparel, furniture and appurtenances], of every name and description, as the same now are lying and being at the port of   , in the said District, and being a vessel of some   tons burthen, and about   feet   inches deep in the hold,

to have and to hold the said granted and described [schooner, her boats, tackle, apparel, furniture and appurtenances], and every part thereof, to the sole and only use, benefit and behoof of the said   , his heirs and assigns forever, as fully and absolutely as I, the said Marshal, under and in virtue of the authority aforesaid, might, could or ought to convey the same.

In witness whereof, I, the said Marshal, have hereunto set my hand and seal, this   day of   , in the year of our Lord one thousand eight hundred and   .

[L. S.]

No. 26.

Marshal's Deed of a Vessel Condemned at the Suit of the United States.

To all to whom these presents shall come, Greeting:

Know ye, that whereas, by virtue of a writ of *venditioni exponas*, issued out of the District Court of the United States of America for the District of   , tested at   , in the said District, the   Tuesday of   , in the year of our Lord one thousand eight hundred and   , directed and delivered to the undersigned, the Marshal of the United States for the District of   , I, the said Marshal, was commanded that I should cause to be sold [the schooner "Adelaide," her boats, tackle, apparel and furniture], in the manner and form by law required, pursuant to a decree made by the said court on the   day of   , 18   , whereby the said [schooner] was condemned to be sold as forfeited to the use of the United States of America for causes and reasons in the said decree stated, the said [schooner] being at the time of the issuing of the aforesaid writ in the custody of the court aforesaid, in virtue of its process theretofore issued, all of which, by reference to the said process and to the libel of information and other proceedings, remaining of record in the said court, will more fully appear. And whereas, after the delivery to me of the said writ of *venditioni exponas*, and before the return day thereof, I did, in obedience to the mandate of the said writ, and in virtue thereof, expose for sale at public action the said [schooner "Adelaide," her boats, tackle, apparel and furniture], at the city of   , in the said District, after having giving due notice of the time and place of such sale, as by law required, and on such sale did strike off and sell the said [schooner "Adelaide," her boats, tackle, apparel and furniture], to   , of   , for the sum of   dollars, that being the best bid, and he being the best bidder therefor, and

which said sale was made on the   day of   ,
A. D. 18 . And whereas, the said   , the purchaser aforesaid, has paid to me, the said Marshal, the sum so bid by him upon such sale as aforesaid.

Now, therefore, know ye, that I, the said Marshal, in virtue of the said writ of *venditioni exponas*, and of the sale so made in pursuance thereof, and of the statute in such case made and provided, and in consideration of the said sum of money so to me paid by the said   , have granted, bargained, sold, conveyed and delivered, and by these presents do grant, bargain, sell, convey and deliver unto the said   , the said [schooner "Adelaide"], together with all and singular, her [boats, tackle, apparel, furniture, and appurtenances], of every name and description, as the same are now lying and being at the port of   , in the said District, to have and to hold the said granted and described [schooner], her [boats, tackle, apparel, furniture and appurtenances], and every part thereof, to the sole and only use, benefit and behoof of the said   , his heirs and assigns forever, as fully and absolutely as I, the Marshal aforesaid, under and in virtue of the authority aforesaid, might, could or ought to convey the same.

In witness whereof, I, the said Marshal, have hereunto set my hand and seal this   day of   , in the year of our Lord one thousand eight hundred and   .

[L. S.]

PART IV.

MISCELLANEOUS FORMS, AND FORMS IN CIVIL AND CRIMINAL CASES.

PART IV.

MISCELLANEOUS FORMS, AND FORMS IN CIVIL AND CRIMINAL CASES.

No. 27.

DEPUTY'S BOND TO MARSHAL.

Know all men by these presents, that we
of   , in the county of   and State
of   , and
are jointly and severally held and firmly bound unto   ,
Marshal of the United States for the District of   , in
the sum of   dollars, good and lawful money of the
United States of America, to be paid to the said   ,
or to his heirs, executors, administrators or assigns, to the
payment of which sum, well and truly to be made, we bind
ourselves, our heirs, executors and administrators, each and
every one, firmly by these presents.

Signed with our hands, and sealed with our seals,
this   day of   , 18 .

Whereas, the said   has this day, by an
instrument in writing, duly executed under his hand and
seal, appointed the said   , Deputy Marshal
of the United States for the District of   : Now,
therefore, the condition of this obligation is such, that if the

above bounden   shall and does legally, fairly, honestly and faithfully perform, execute and discharge all the duties of the said office of Deputy Marshal, and all acts and things pertaining thereto or connected therewith, and shall at all times pay over to the said   , or to such other person or persons, court or officer as of right the same shall belong, all damages, costs, fines, fees, sum or sums of money that shall be collected or received by him as such Deputy Marshal; and shall in all things and at all times indemnify and save harmless the said   , as such Marshal, for, touching and in any wise concerning the due execution and return of all writs and process that shall come to the hands of the said   , as such Deputy Marshal, and also for and concerning all, any and every escape that the said   , as such Deputy Marshal, shall or may suffer, whether the same be negligent or voluntary, and of and from the payment of all damages, costs, trouble, counsel charges and expense which the said   may be charged with, subject to, or in any manner become liable to pay for, on account of, or by reason of any act or thing of the said   , in relation to the said office of Deputy Marshal, either of omission or commission or otherwise; and also, if the said   shall duly and faithfully furnish and forward to the said   , Marshal, as aforesaid, within three days after the receipt of each and every process which he may receive from any person than the said   , the title of the cause and the name and address of the attorney or proctor who shall issue the same, together with the time of service thereof, when served, and make return to the said Marshal of all process served by the said   , and pay to the said Marshal all money collected on execution or otherwise without delay, that the Marshal can make the appropriate returns to the Clerk's office; and shall, at the time of noticing any and every sale of any property, at the same time send to the said Marshal notice of such sale, and also notify him of all

MISCELLANEOUS FORMS. 123

adjournments of sale, and shall also in all things well and truly observe and follow the instructions of said Marshal; then this obligation to be void and of no effect, and otherwise to remain in full force and virtue.

Sealed and delivered }
   in presence of

UNITED STATES OF AMERICA, } *ss.*
   DISTRICT OF ,

Be it remembered, that on this   day of   ,
18 , personally came before me

and severally acknowledged that they executed the foregoing bond; and I certify that they are the same persons described in and who executed said bond.

UNITED STATES OF AMERICA, } *ss.*
   DISTRICT OF ,

being severally sworn, depose and say, each for himself, that he is a resident and freeholder in the State of   ,
and worth the sum of   thousand dollars, over and above all his debts and liabilities.

Subscribed and sworn this   day }
   of   , 18 , before me.

No. 28.

RETURN TO CRIMINAL CAPIAS, OR WARRANT TO APPREHEND.

Defendant arrested.

I certify, that on the   day of   , 18 , at   , in my District, I arrested the within named defendant, and have him here in my custody, as I am within commanded.

Dated   .

                                        , U. S. Marshal,

          by   , Deputy,

No. 29.

RETURN TO CRIMINAL CAPIAS.

One of the Defendants arrested.

I certify, that on the   day of   , 18 , at   , in my District, I arrested the within named   , and have him here in my custody, as I am within commanded; but I am unable to find the within named   in my District.

Dated   .

                                        , U. S. Marshal.

          by   , Deputy.

MISCELLANEOUS FORMS. 125

No. 30.

RETURN TO CRIMINAL CAPIAS.

Defendant not found.

I certify, that after diligent search, I am unable to find the within named   in my District, so that I may have him before this court, as I am within commanded.

Dated   .

                              , *U. S. Marshal.*
         by   , *Deputy.*

No. 31.

DISCLAIMER.

U. S.   COURT, DISTRICT OF   .

The U. S. of America

v.

John Doe.

The defendant was indicted at the   term, 18 , of said court, held at   , in said District, for the offense of [here state the offense mentioned in the capias].
        , 18 . Received criminal capias issued out of said court, tested the   Tuesday of   , 18 , and returnable the   Tuesday of   , 18 , at   .

The defendant [John Doe] was found in the District of   . Deputy Marshal   was deputed by the Marshal of said District of   to arrest the

said defendant and convey him to the District of   ,
to be further dealt with according to law.

I,   , Marshal of the United States for the District of   , do hereby disclaim, in favor of   , Marshal for the District of   , all my right and title in and to the fees and service of process in the above entitled case; and to the transportation of said defendant under said process; and I hereby authorize payment thereof to be made to the said Marshal   .

Dated   18   .

            , U. S. Marshal,

            District of   .

No. 32.

RETURN TO BAILABLE CAPIAS.

Defendant arrested and committed.

I certify that, on the   day of   , 18   , at   , in my District, I arrested the within named   , and have committed him to the county jail of   county, in default of bail.

Dated   .

            , U. S. Marshal,

            by   , *Deputy*.

Service, $.

Travel,   miles, at   c. per mile, $.

MISCELLANEOUS FORMS.

No. 33.

RETURN TO BAILABLE CAPIAS.

Defendant arrested and discharged on bail.

I certify that, on the   day   , 18 , at   , in my District, I arrested the within named   , and having received a bond conditioned that he shall put in special bail within twenty days after the return day hereof; and, if required, shall perfect such bail, I immediately discharged him from arrest.

Dated   .

                              , *U. S. Marshal*,
            by   , *Deputy*.

Service, $.
Travel,   miles, at   c. per mile, $.
Bond, $.

No. 34.

BOND TO MARSHAL.

On discharging a defendant arrested on Bailable Capias.

Know all men by these presents, That we   , of   , as principal, and   of   , as sureties, are held and bound unto   , United States Marshal for the District of   , in the sum of   dollars, lawful money of the United States, to be paid to the said   , or to his certain attorney, executors, administrators or assigns, for the payment of which, well and truly to be made, we jointly and severally bind ourselves, our heirs, executors and administrators firmly by these presents.

Sealed with our seals and dated this   day of   , 18 .

The condition of this obligation is such, That if the above named   , who has been arrested upon a certain writ of *capias ad respondendum*, issued out of the   Court of the United States for the   District of   , returnable the   Tuesday of   , 18 , before the said court at   , requiring the said   to answer unto the United States of America, in a plea of trespass; and also to a certain bill of the said United States against the said   , for   [here insert the cause of action mentioned in the capias],   shall appear in this action, commenced as above recited, by putting in special bail twenty days after the return day specified in said writ, and if required shall perfect such bail according to the rules and practice of the said court, then the above obligation to be void; otherwise, to remain in full force and virtue.

DISTRICT OF   , *ss:*

          , being duly sworn, each for himself, says: That he resides in the county of   , in said District, and that he is a freeholder and worth the sum of   over and above all his debts and liabilities.

Subscribed and sworn before me, }
  this   day of   , 18 , }

          ,
United States Commissioner.

MISCELLANEOUS FORMS. 129

DISTRICT OF , ss :

On this day of , 18 , before me personally came , to me known to be the persons described in and who executed the within instrument, and severally acknowledged that they executed the same for the uses and purposes therein stated.

United States Commissioner.

No. 35.

RETURN TO NON-BAILABLE CAPIAS.

Defendant served.

I certify, that on the day of , 18 , at , in my District, I personally served the within writ on , the within defendant, by showing to him the same, with the seal of the court thereon, and at the same time delivering to him a copy thereof.

Dated .

, *U. S. Marshal*,

by , *Deputy.*

Service, $.

Travel, miles, at c. per mile, $.

No. 36.

RETURN TO CAPIAS.

Defendant not found.

I certify, that after diligent search, I am unable to find the within named   in my District.

Dated

, *U. S. Marshal*,

by   , *Deputy*.

No. 37.

MARSHAL'S BILL — CIVIL SUIT.

DISTRICT COURT OF THE UNITED STATES
FOR THE   DISTRICT OF

The United States

v.

Richard Roe.

Serving capias at   , ret. at   ,........ $2 00
Travel to return the same,   miles, at six cents,..
Bond, ... 50
Discharging defendant,.......................... 50
Oath and certificate disbursements,................ 25
Serving writ of inquiry at 5 00

Taxed at $ this   day }
  of   , 18 .   }
                , *Clerk.*

MISCELLANEOUS FORMS. 131

UNITED STATES OF AMERICA, } ss.
NORTHERN DISTRICT OF NEW YORK.

, Marshal of the said District, being duly sworn, deposes and says, that the services charged in the foregoing bill have been actually and necessarily performed as therein stated, and that the expenses mentioned in said bill have been actually and necessarily incurred as therein set forth.

Subscribed and sworn before me }
this   day of   , 18 .

, *U. S. Commissioner.*

No. 38.

RETURN TO SUMMONS.

Served.

I certify, that on the   day of   , 18 , at   , in my District, I personally served the within summons on   , the within defendant [or, " on   , the president, cashier or secretary, as the case may be, of the within mentioned   "], by showing to him the same, with the seal of the court thereon, and at the same time delivering to him a copy thereof.

Dated   .

, *U. S. Marshal.*

by   , *Deputy.*

Service, $.

Travel,   miles, at   c. per mile, $.

No. 39.

Return to Writ of Subpœna in Equity.

I certify, that on the   day of   , 18 , at   , in my District, I personally served the within writ on the within named   , by [showing to him the same, with the seal of the court thereon, and leaving with him a copy thereof], or [by leaving a copy thereof, at his usual place of abode, with a member of his family].

Dated   .

, *U. S. Marshal*,

by   , *Deputy.*

Service, $.

Travel,   miles, at   c. per mile, $

No. 40.

Return to Writ of Certiorari.

I certify, that on the   day of   , 18 , at   , in my District, I personally served the within writ on [here insert the name and official title of the person on whom service is made], by showing to him the same, with the seal of the court thereon, and at the same time delivering to him a copy thereof.

Dated   .

, *U. S. Marshal*,

by   , *Deputy.*

Service, $.

Travel,   miles, at   c. per mile, $.

MISCELLANEOUS FORMS. 133

No. 41.

RETURN TO VENIRE.

The answer of   , Marshal of the United States
for the District of   .

The execution of this precept appears by the panels hereto annexed.

Dated   .

, *U. S. Marshal*,

by   , *Deputy*.

No. 42.

CERTIFICATE TO JURY PANELS.

We, the undersigned,   , Deputy Marshal of the United States for the District of   , and   , County Clerk of the county of   [or, Clerk of the U. S. Circuit, or Clerk of the U. S. District Court for the District of   ], do hereby certify the foregoing to be a panel of grand jurors, and a panel of petit jurors, by us duly drawn, at the office of the Clerk of the county of   , on the   day of   , 18   .

, *Deputy Marshal*.

, *Clerk of*   .

134 MISCELLANEOUS FORMS.

No. 43.

NOTICE TO JURORS.

Mr.   :

SIR: You are hereby summoned to attend a   Court of the United States, held for the District of   , at the [court house] in the   of   , in the county of   , on the   day of   18   , at 10 o'clock A. M., as a [grand or petit] juror.

Dated   , 18 .

            , U. S. Marshal,

       by   , Deputy.

No. 44.

RETURN TO SUBPŒNA.

Personally served on   , at   , this   day of   , 18 .

Travel thereon, one way,   miles.

            , U. S. Marshal,

       by   , Deputy.

No. 45.

SUBPŒNA TICKET — U. S. CASES.

To   :

SIR: By virtue of a subpœna, issued out of the   Court of the United States for the District of   , and herewith shown unto you, you are required to appear and be before the said court, at the [court house] in the   of   , on [Tuesday], the   day

MISCELLANEOUS FORMS. 135

of   , 18   , at 10 o'clock in the forenoon, on behalf of the United States, and not to depart said court without leave. If you fail to obey such subpœna, you may be fined and imprisoned, as the court shall direct.

                                , *U. S. Marshal.*
              by   , *Deputy.*

No. 46.

SUBPŒNA TICKET — SUITS BETWEEN PRIVATE PARTIES.

To   :

SIR: By virtue of a subpœna, issued out of the   Court of the United States for the District of   , in a certain suit pending therein, wherein   is the plaintiff and   is the defendant, and herewith shown unto you, you are required to appear and be before the said court, at the [court house] in the city of   , on the   day of   , 18   , at 10 o'clock in the forenoon, on behalf of the said [plaintiff]. If you fail to obey such subpœna, you may be fined and imprisoned, as the court shall direct.

                                , *U. S. Marshal,*
              by   , *Deputy.*

No. 47.

NOTICE TO BE INDORSED ON SUBPŒNA TICKET — U. S. CASES.

TAKE NOTICE: You will (if you appear at the place and hour appointed, and continue in court) be entitled to $1.50 per day for attendance, and five cents per mile each way for necessary travel; but if you are called on the first or any other day, either in the forenoon or afternoon, and fail to answer, your fees for the day may be deducted, and a fine imposed on you by the court.

No. 48.

RECEIPT FOR PRISONER.

Received of   , U. S. Marshal for the District of   , this   day of   , 18   , the body of the within named.

[Name and official title of officer.]

No. 49.

RETURN TO ATTACHMENT AGAINST WITNESS.

I have arrested the within named   , as I am within commanded, and have him now here before the court.

Dated   .

, *U. S. Marshal,*

by   , *Deputy.*

Service, $.

Travel,   miles, at   c. per mile, $.

No. 50.

SPECIAL DEPUTIZATION.

I hereby depute and authorize   , of   , to execute the within writ.

Dated   , 18 .

, *U. S. Marshal.*

MISCELLANEOUS FORMS. 137

No. 51.

OATH TO JURORS ON WRIT OF INQUIRY.

You, and each of yon, do swear [or, affirm], that you will well and truly inquire and determine the amount of debt due from   to   , and true inquisition make, according to the evidence, so help you God.

No. 52.

OATH TO WITNESS ON WRIT OF INQUIRY.

You do swear [or, affirm], that the evidence you shall give in the matter in difference between   and   , shall be the truth, the whole truth, and nothing but the truth, so help you God.

No. 53.

RETURN TO WRIT OF INQUIRY.

I certify, that on the   day of   , 18 , at   , in my District, I executed the within writ, as appears by the inquisition hereto annexed.

Dated   .

, *U. S. Marshal*,

by   , *Deputy*.

No. 54.

INQUISITION.

DISTRICT OF   , ss :

An inquisition indented and taken at   , in the city of   , in the District of   , on the   day of   , 18 , before me,   , Marshal of the United States for the District of   , by virtue of a writ to me directed, and to this inquisition annexed, by the oaths of   [here insert the names of the jurors], good and lawful men of the said District, who being charged and sworn say, upon their oaths, that [here insert the name of the plaintiff], in the said writ named, hath sustained damages, occasioned by reason of the premises therein contained, besides his costs and charges by him about his suit in this behalf expended, the sum of   dollars ($).

In witness whereof, as well as I, the said   , Marshal, as the jurors aforesaid, our names and seals to this inquisition have severally put, the day and year aforesaid.

             , *U. S. Marshal.* [L. S.]

[Signatures and seals of the twelve jurors.]

No. 55.

RETURN TO EXECUTION.

Satisfied.

I have collected on the within execution the sum of   dollars ($) and my fees.

Dated   .

             , *U. S. Marshal,*

             by   , *Deputy.*

MISCELLANEOUS FORMS. 139

No. 56.

RETURN TO EXECUTION.

Part made and Nulla Bona as to residue.

I have collected the sum of dollars ($), part of the moneys directed to be made upon the within execution ; and I can find no goods or chattels, lands or tenements of the within defendant in my District, whereof I can make the balance of the said execution.

Dated   .

, *U. S. Marshal*,

by   *Deputy.*

No. 57.

RETURN TO EXECUTION.

Nulla Bona.

I have made diligent search, and can find no goods or chattels, lands or tenements, of the within defendant, in my District, whereof I can make the amount of the within execution or any part thereof.

Dated   .

, *U. S. Marshal*,

by   *Deputy.*

No. 58.

RETURN TO EXECUTION AGAINST AN EXECUTOR OR ADMINISTRATOR.

Nulla Bona.

The within defendant has no goods or chattels, which were of the within named deceased at the time of his death, in his hands to be administered in my District, whereof I can cause to be made the amount of the within execution, or any part thereof.

Dated

, *U. S. Marshal,*

by *Deputy.*

No. 59.

INDORSEMENT OF LEVY.

Levied this   day of   , 18 , at   o'clock   . M., on the following property, under and by virtue of the within execution, at the city of   , viz.: [here describe the property levied on.]

, *U. S. Marshal,*

by , *Deputy.*

No. 60.

INDORSEMENT OF LEVY.

When the articles are too numerous to indorse on the execution, describe the same in a schedule, which may be marked " A," and annex it to the execution as follows:

U. S.   COURT, DISTRICT OF

The U. S. of America
    v.
John Doe.

Levied this   day of   , 18 , at   o'clock . M., on the following property, under and by virtue of the within execution, at the city of   , viz.: [here describe the property levied on.]

                          , *U. S. Marshal,*
              by   , *Deputy.*

The following indorsement should then be made on the execution, viz.:

I have levied on the property mentioned in the annexed schedule, marked "A," under the within execution, as therein stated.

                          , *U. S. Marshal,*
              by   , *Deputy.*

No. 61.

RECEIPT FOR PROPERTY LEVIED ON.

U. S.   COURT, DISTRICT OF

The U. S. of America
    v.
John Doe.

Execution for $, and interest from   , besides Marshal's fees, received by me,   , 18   , for execution.

I have levied upon the following property in the possession of the defendant at   , under said execution, viz.: [here specify the property levied on.]

                                        , *U. S. Marshal,*
               by   , *Deputy.*

I hereby acknowledge that I have received the above described property, so levied upon by the Marshal of the District of   , from said Marshal, and hereby promise and undertake to return the same and every part thereof to the said Marshal, on demand, or pay the above judgment, interest and Marshal's fees.

Dated

No. 62.

NOTICE OF SALE OF PERSONAL PROPERTY.

By virtue of an execution, issued out of the   Court of the United States of America for the District of   , and to me directed and delivered, I have levied on and taken all the right, title and interest of   , of, in and to the following property, to wit: [here describe the property], which I shall expose for sale at public vendue, as the law directs, on [Tuesday], the   day of   , 18   , at   o'clock in the   noon, at   , in the city of   .

Dated

                                        , *U. S. Marshal,*
               by   , *Deputy.*

MISCELLANEOUS FORMS. 143

No. 63.

NOTICE OF SALE OF REAL ESTATE.

By virtue of an execution, issued out of the   Court of the United States of America for the District of   , against the goods and chattels, lands and tenements of   , I have seized all the right and title of the said   , of, in and to the following described premises, to wit: [here describe the property], which I shall expose for sale, as the law directs, on [Tuesday], the   day of   , 18 , at   o'clock in the   noon, at   , in the city of   .

Dated   .

, *U. S. Marshal*,

by   , *Deputy*.

No. 64.

RETURN TO CA. SA.

Debt satisfied.

I certify, that on the   day of   , 18 , at   , in my District, I arrested the within named   , and committed him to the common jail of   county. Subsequently, the said   having paid to me the sum of   dollars ($), being the amount of said fine [or judgment], and the interest thereon, besides my fees and expenses hereon, I immediately discharged him from arrest.

Dated   .

, *U. S. Marshal*,

by   , *Deputy*.

144   MISCELLANEOUS FORMS.

No. 65.

RETURN TO CA. SA.

Defendant arrested and committed.

I certify, that on the   day of   , 18   ,
at   , in my District, I arrested the within
named   , and have committed him to the
common jail of   county.

Dated   .

, *U. S. Marshal,*

by   , *Deputy.*

Service, $.

Travel,   miles, at   c. per mile.

No. 66.

WARRANT OF DISTRICT JUDGE FOR THE REMOVAL OF A PRISONER COMMITTED BY A UNITED STATES COMMISSIONER.

The President of the United States of America, to the Marshal of the United States for the District of   , and to his Deputies whomsoever, GREETING :

Whereas,   has been charged before   , Esq., a commissioner duly appointed by the Circuit Court of the United States for the District of   , with having committed an offense against the laws of the United States, in this, that on the   day of   , A. D. 18   , at   , in the District of   , the said   did [here state the offense mentioned in the commissioner's commitment]. And after an examination of the witnesses against the said   , it appearing to the said commissioner that the said offense has been committed, and that there is probable cause to believe the said ,   to be guilty of the offense thus charged. And the said   , not having offered sufficient bail for his appearance at the next court having cognizance of such offense, to answer therefor, was by the said commissioner committed to the common jail of the county of   , for want of sureties, and until he should be discharged by due course of law, or be removed into the District where said offense was committed; and whereas, also, the said   still remains, and now is, in the said common jail of the county of   , in the District of   , pursuant to the aforesaid commitment, and is unable to give bail; you are, therefore, hereby commanded, that you take the body of the said   forthwith, if he shall still be in custody under said commitment, and deliver him into the custody of the Marshal of the United States for the said District of   , that being the District in which the alleged offense was committed, to be there dealt with according to law; and do you make return what you shall have done, together with this writ, to the clerk of the said District of [here insert the name of the District into which the prisoner is to be removed].

In testimony whereof, I have hereunto set my hand and seal at   , in the District of   , this   day of   , A. D. 18   , and of the Independence of the United States the   .

[L. S.]

District Judge of the United States for the District of   .

146 MISCELLANEOUS FORMS.

No. 67.

Marshal's Return to above Warrant.

I hereby certify, that in obedience to the within writ, I did, on the   day of   , A. D. 18 , at   , in my District, take the body of the within named   , and on the same day [or any subsequent day] did transport and deliver him into the custody of the United States Marshal for the District of   , at   .

, *Marshal*,

by   , *Deputy*.

Service, $.

Travel,   miles.

No. 68.

Solicitor's Distress Warrant.

To   Esq., United States Marshal for the District of   . Whereas,   , late [official title], in relation to his several accounts, stands indebted to the United States in a cash balance of   dollars, as appears by the settlement of his said accounts, made by the proper accounting officers of the treasury, a copy of which is herewith inclosed; and whereas the said   , having failed to pay over according to the act of Congress, passed the 15th day of May, 1820, entitled "An act for the better organization of the treasury department," the said sum of   dollars, these are, therefore, in pursuance of said act, to command you to proceed immediately to levy and collect the said sum of   dollars, by distress and sale of the goods and chattels of the said   , giving ten days previous notice of such intended sale, by affixing an advertisement of the articles to be sold at two or more public places in the town or county where the said goods or chattels were taken, or in the town or county where the owner of such goods and chattels may reside; and should there not be found sufficient goods and chattels to satisfy the said sum of   dollars remaining due and unpaid as aforesaid, you are hereby commanded to commit the body of the said   to prison, there to remain until discharged by due course of law; and should the said   be committed to prison, as aforesaid, or if he abscond, and goods and chattels sufficient to satisfy the said sum of   dollars, be not found, you are hereby commanded to levy upon, and expose to sale, at public auction, for cash, to the highest bidder, the lands, tenements and hereditaments of the said   , or so much thereof as may be necessary to satisfy the said sum of   dollars, or whatever sum there may remain due and unpaid thereof, after you shall have given notice of the said sale, at least three weeks prior to its taking place, in not less than three public places in the county or district where such real estate is situate; and all moneys which may remain of the proceeds of such sale, after satisfying the said sum of   dollars, and paying the reasonable costs and charges of the sale, you are required to return to the proprietor or proprietors of the land or real estate sold as aforesaid; and whatever you may do in obedience to this warrant, make return thereof to this office; and for so doing this shall be your sufficient authority.

Given under my hand and seal at my office, in the Treasury Department at Washington, this   day of   , A. D., 18 .

Solicitor of the Treasury.

APPENDIX (A).

APPENDIX (A).

FEE BILL.

In lieu of the compensation now allowed by law to attorneys, solicitors and proctors in the United States courts, to United States district attorneys, clerks of the district and circuit courts, marshals, witnesses, jurors, commissioners, and printers, in the several States, the following and no other compensation shall be taxed and allowed. But this act shall not be construed to prohibit attorneys, solicitors and proctors from charging to and receiving from their clients, other than the government, such reasonable compensation for their services, in addition to the taxable costs, as may be in accordance with general usage in their respective States, or may be agreed upon between the parties.

FEES OF ATTORNEYS, SOLICITORS, AND PROCTORS.

In a trial before a jury, in civil and criminal causes, or before referees, or on a final hearing in equity or admiralty, a docket fee of twenty dollars: *Provided*, that in cases in admiralty and maritime jurisdiction, where the libellant shall recover less than fifty dollars, the docket fee of his proctor shall be but ten dollars.

In cases at law, where judgment is rendered without a jury, ten dollars; and five dollars where a cause is discontinued.

For scire facias and other proceedings on recognizances, five dollars.

For each deposition taken and admitted as evidence in the cause, two dollars and fifty cents.

A compensation of five dollars shall be allowed for the services rendered in cases removed from a district to a circuit court, by writ of error or appeal. (Act Feb. 26, 1853, 10 Stat. at L. 161.)

DISTRICT ATTORNEY'S FEES.

For examination by a district attorney, before a judge or commissioner, of a person or persons charged with crime, five dollars per day for the time necessarily employed.

For each day of his necessary attendance in a court of the United States, on the business of the United States, when the same shall be held at the place of his abode, five dollars, and the like sum for his attendance for each day of the term when the said court shall be held elsewhere.

For traveling, from the place of his abode to the place of holding any court of the United States in his district, and to the place of any examination before a judge or commissioner, of a person or persons charged with crime, ten cents per mile for going, and ten cents for returning.

When an indictment for crime shall be tried before a jury, and a conviction is had, in addition to the attorney's fees allowed by this act, the district attorney may be allowed a counsel fee in proportion to the importance and difficulty of the cause, not exceeding thirty dollars.

For the services of counsel, rendered at the request of the head of a department, such sum as may be stipulated or agreed on. (Act Feb. 26, 1853, 10 Stat. at L. 162.)

There shall be taxed and paid to district attorneys two per centum upon all moneys collected or realized in any suit or proceeding arising under the revenue laws conducted by them in which the United States is a party. The act in relation to costs, approved February 26th, 1853, shall not apply to such allowances, and the same shall be in lieu of all costs and fees in such suit or proceedings. (Act March 3, 1863, 12 Stat. at L. 741, § 11.)

APPENDIX (A). 153

CLERKS' FEES.

For issuing and entering every process, commission, summons, capias, execution, warrant, attachment or other writ, except a writ of venire, summons or subpœna for a witness, one dollar.

For filing and entering every declaration, plea or other paper, ten cents.

For administering every oath or affirmation to a witness or other person, except a juror, ten cents.

For entering any return, rule, order, continuance, judgment, decree or recognizance, drawing any bond or making any record, certificate, return or report, for each folio, fifteen cents; and for a copy of any such entry or record, or of any paper on file, not exceeding one folio, ten cents; and for each additional folio, ten cents.

For making dockets and indexes, and for all other services on the trial or argument of a cause where issue is joined and testimony given, including venire and taxing costs, three dollars.

For making dockets and indexes, and for all other services in a cause where issue is joined and no testimony given, including taxing costs, two dollars.

For making dockets and indexes, and for taxing costs and other services in a cause which is dismissed, discontinued, or a judgment or decree is made or rendered therein without issue, one dollar.

In equity and admiralty causes only, the process, pleadings and decree, and such orders and memoranda as may be necessary to show the jurisdiction of the court and regularity of the proceedings, shall be entered upon the final record; and, in case of an appeal, copies of the proofs, and of such entries and papers on file as may be necessary on hearing of the appeal, may be certified up to the appellate court.

For affixing a seal of the court to any instrument when required, twenty cents. For issuing a writ of subpœna, twenty-five cents. For every search for any particular mortgage, judgment or other lien, fifteen cents. For traveling from the office of the clerk, where he is required by law to reside, to the place of holding any court required to be held by law, five cents per mile for going and five for returning, and five dollars per day for his attendance on any such court or courts while actually in session.

For searching the records of the court for judgments, decrees and other instruments constituting a general lien upon real estate, and certifying the result of such search, fifteen cents for each person against whom such search is required to be made.

For receiving, keeping and paying out money, in pursuance of the requirements of any statute or order of court, one per cent on the amount so received, kept and paid.

In cases removed by writ of error or appeal, the clerk's fees for making dockets and taxing costs, shall be but one dollar; and the clerks of the district and circuit courts respectively, *ex officio*, shall be, and hereby are, authorized and empowered to administer oaths, take acknowledgments, take and certify affidavits and depositions in the same manner as commissioners, and shall be entitled to the same fees and compensation therefor. (Act Feb. 26, 1853, 10 Stat. at L. 163.)

Marshals' Fees.

For service of any warrant, attachment, summons, capias or other writ (except execution, venire or a summons or subpœna for a witness), two dollars for each person on whom such service may be made: *Provided*, that on petition, setting forth the facts on oath, the court may allow such fair compensation for the keeping of personal property attached and held on mesne process, as shall on examination be found to be reasonable.

For serving a writ of subpœna on a witness, fifty cents; and no further compensation shall be allowed for any copy, summons or notice for witness.

For travel in going only to serve any process, warrant, attachment or other writ, including writs of subpœna in civil and criminal cases, six cents per mile, to be computed from the place of service to the court or place where the writ or process is returned; and if more than one person is served therewith, the travel shall be computed from the court to the place of service which shall be the most remote, adding thereto the extra travel which shall be necessary to serve it on the other: *Provided*, that when more than two writs of any kind in behalf of the same party or parties, to be served on the same person or persons, or part of the same persons, are or might be served at the same time, the Marshal shall be entitled to compensation for travel on only two of such writs. And to save unnecessary expense, it shall be the duty of the clerk to insert the names of as many witnesses in a cause in such subpœna as convenience in serving the same will permit. And, in all cases where mileage is allowed to the Marshal by this act, it shall be at his option to receive the same, or his actual traveling expenses, to be proved on his oath to the satisfaction of the court.

For each bail bond, fifty cents.

For summoning appraisers, each fifty cents.

For every commitment or discharge of a prisoner, fifty cents.

For every proclamation in admiralty, thirty cents.

For sales of vessels or other property, under process in admiralty, or under the order of a court of admiralty, and for receiving and paying the money, for any sum under five hundred dollars, two and one-half per centum; for any larger sum, one and one-quarter per centum upon the excess.

For serving an attachment *in rem*, or a libel in admiralty, two dollars; and the necessary expenses of keeping boats, vessels or other property attached or libeled in admiralty, not exceeding two dollars and fifty cents per day; and, in case the debt or claim shall be settled by the parties without a sale of the property, the Marshal shall be entitled to a commission of one per cent on the first five hundred dollars of the claim or decree, and one-half of one per cent on the excess over five hundred dollars: *Provided*, that in case the value of the property shall be less than the claim, then, and in such case, such commission shall be allowed only on the appraised value thereof.

For serving a writ of possession, partition, execution or any final process, the same mileage as is herein allowed for the service of any other writ; and for making the service, seizing or levying on property, advertising and disposing of the same by sale, set-off, or otherwise, according to law, receiving and paying over the money, the same fees and poundage as are or shall be allowed for similar services to the sheriffs of the several States, respectively, in which the service may be rendered.

For serving venires and summoning every twelve men as grand or petit jurors, four dollars, or thirty-three and one-third cents each; and in those States where jurors, by the laws of the State, are drawn by constables or other officers of corporate towns or places by lot, the Marshal shall receive for the use of the officers employed in drawing and summoning the jurors and returning each venire, two dollars; and for his own trouble in distributing the venires, two dollars for each jury: *Provided*, that in no case shall the fees for distributing and serving venires, and drawing and summoning jurors by township officers, including mileage chargeable by the Marshal for such service, at any court, exceed fifty dollars.

For traveling from his residence to the place of holding court, to attend a term thereof, ten cents per mile for going only, and five dollars per day for attending the circuit and district courts when they are both in session, or for attending either of said courts when but one is in session, and for bringing in and committing prisoners and witnesses during the term.

For executing a deed prepared by a party or his attorney, one dollar.

For drawing and executing a deed, five dollars.

For transporting criminals, ten cents per mile for himself, each necessary guard, and each prisoner.

For copies of writs or papers furnished at the request of any party, ten cents per folio.

For holding a court of inquiry or other proceedings before a jury, including the summoning of a jury, five dollars.

The Marshal of the District of South Carolina shall hereafter be entitled to receive a salary of two hundred dollars per annum.

The respective courts of the United States shall appoint criers for their courts, to be allowed the sum of two dollars per day; and the Marshals are hereby authorized to appoint such a number of persons, not exceeding five, as the judges of their respective courts shall determine, to attend upon the grand and other juries, and for other necessary purposes, who shall be allowed for their services the sum of two dollars per day, to be paid by and included in the accounts of the Marshal, out of any money of the United States in his hands; the compensation to be given only for actual attendance; and when both courts are in session at the same time, to be paid but for attendance on one court.

For expenses while employed in endeavoring to arrest, under process, any person charged with or convicted of a crime, the sum actually expended, not to exceed two dollars per day, in addition to his compensation for service and travel.

For disbursing money to jurors and witnesses, and for other expenses, two per centum.

For attending examinations before a commissioner, and bringing in, guarding and returning prisoners charged with crime, and witnesses, two dollars per day, and the same for each Deputy necessarily attending, not exceeding two.

SEC. 2. *And be it further enacted*, that there shall be paid to the Marshal his fees for services rendered for the United States, for summoning jurors, and witnesses in behalf of the United States, and in behalf of any prisoner to be tried for a capital offense; for the maintenance of prisoners of the United States confined in jail for any criminal offense; for the commitment or discharge of such prisoners; for the expenses necessarily incurred for fuel, lights and other contingencies that may accrue in holding the courts within the district, and providing the books necessary to record the proceedings thereof: *Provided*, that the Marshal shall not incur an expense of more than twenty dollars in any one year for furniture, or fifty dollars for rent of building and making improvements thereon, without first submitting a statement and estimates to the Secretary of the Interior, and getting his instructions in the premises.

SEC. 3. *And be it further enacted*, that every district atttorney, clerk of a district court, clerk of a circuit court, and Marshal of the United States, shall, until otherwise directed by law, upon the first day of January and July, in each year, commencing with the first day of July next, or within thirty days from and after the days specified, make to the Secretary of the Interior, in such form as he shall prescribe, a return in writing, embracing all the fees and emoluments of their respective offices, of every name and character, distinguishing the fees and emoluments received or payable under the bankrupt act from those received or payable for any other service; and in the case of a Marshal, further distinguishing the fees and emoluments received or payable for services by himself personally rendered from those received or payable for services rendered by a Deputy; and also distinguishing the fees and emoluments so received or payable for services rendered by each Deputy, by name, and the proportion of such fees and emoluments which, by the terms of his service, each Deputy is to receive; and also embracing all the necessary office expenses of such officer, together with the vouchers for the payment of the same, for the half year ending on the said first day of January or July, as the case may be; which return shall be, in all cases, verified by the oath of the officer making the same; * * * * and no Marshal shall be allowed by the said Secretary to retain, of the fees and emoluments of his office, for his own personal compensation, over and above a proper allowance to his Deputies,

APPENDIX (A). 159

which shall in no case exceed three-fourths of the fees and emoluments received as payable for the services rendered by the Deputy to whom the allowance is made, and may be reduced below that rate by the said Secretary of the Interior, whenever the return shall show that rate of allowance to be unreasonable, and over and above the necessary office expenses of the said Marshal, the necessary clerk hire included, also to be audited and allowed by the proper accounting officers of the treasury, a sum exceeding six thousand dollars per year, or at and after that rate for such times as he shall hold the office; and every such officer shall, with each such return made by him, pay into the treasury of the United States, or deposit to the credit of the Treasurer thereof, as he may be directed by the Secretary of the Interior, any surplus of the fees and emoluments of his office, which his half-yearly return so made as aforesaid shall show to exist, over and above the compensation and allowances hereinbefore authorized to be retained and paid by him. And in every case where the return of any such officer shall show that a surplus may exist, the said Secretary of the Interior shall cause such returns to be carefully examined, and the accounts of disbursements to be regularly audited by the proper officers of his department, and an account to be opened with such officer, in proper books to be provided for that purpose; and the allowances for personal compensation for each calendar year shall be made from the fees and emoluments of that year, and not otherwise: *And provided, further*, that nothing in any existing law of Congress, authorizing the payment of a per diem compensation to a district attorney, clerk of a district court, or clerk of a circuit court, or Marshal, or Deputy Marshal, for attendance upon the district or circuit courts during their sittings, shall be so construed as to authorize any such payment to any one of those officers for attendance upon either of those courts while sitting for the transaction of business under the bankrupt law merely, or for any portion of the time for which either of the said courts may be held open or in session by the authority conferred in that law;

and no such charge in an account of any such officer shall be certified as payable, or shall be allowed and paid out of the money hereinbefore appropriated for defraying the expenses of the courts of the United States. And no per diem or other allowance shall be made to any such officer for attendance at rule days of the circuit or district courts; and when the circuit and district courts sit at the same time, no greater per diem or other allowance shall be made to any such officer than for an attendance on one court.   *   *   *   *   *

The bill of fees of clerk, Marshal and attorneys, and the amount paid printers and witnessess, and lawful fees for exemplifications and copies of papers necessarily obtained for use on trial in cases where by law costs are recoverable in favor of the prevailing party, shall be taxed by a judge or clerk of the court, and be included in and form a portion of a judgment or decree against the losing party. Such taxed bills shall be filed with the papers in the cause.

In cases where the United States are parties, the Marshal shall, on the order of the court, to be entered in its minutes, pay to the jurors and witnesses all such fees as they may appear by such order to be entitled to, which sums shall be allowed him at the treasury in his accounts.

The fees of the Marshals, clerks, commissioners and district attorneys, in cases where the United States are liable to pay the same, shall be paid on settling their accounts at the treasury, such accounts to be made out and verified by the party under oath, and forwarded to the First Auditor of the Treasury.

In prize cases, where there is a condemnation and sale, the costs, so far as they are payable and can be paid out of the proceeds of sale, shall be paid on the order of the court upon the filing of the taxed bills, making them a portion of the record in the case.

No district attorney, Marshal or clerk, or their deputies, shall receive any other or greater compensation for any services rendered by him than is provided in this act; and all acts and parts of acts, allowing to either of them any other or greater fees than is herein provided, are hereby repealed, and to receive any other or greater compensation is hereby declared to be a misdemeanor. And if any officer hereinbefore mentioned, or his deputy, shall, by reason or cover of his office, willfully and corruptly demand and receive any other or greater fees than those allowed in this act, he shall, on conviction thereof in any court of the United States, forfeit and pay a fine not exceeding five hundred dollars, and be imprisoned not exceeding six months, at the discretion of the court before whom the conviction shall be had. But this shall not be construed to prohibit the payment of any salary authorized by statute. * *

That before any bill of costs shall be taxed by any judge or other officer, or allowed by any officer of the treasury, in favor of clerks, Marshals, commissioners or district attorneys, the party claiming such bill shall prove by his own oath, or, some other person having a knowledge of the facts, to be attached to such bill, and filed therewith, that the services charged therein have been actually and necessarily performed, as therein stated. * *

SEC. 4. *And be it further enacted*, that if any person shall falsely take an oath or affirmation in relation to any matter authorized by this act, such person shall be deemed guilty of perjury, and upon conviction thereof shall suffer the pains and penalties in that case provided.

SEC. 5. *And be it further enacted*, that all laws and regulations heretofore made, which are imcompatible with the provisions of this act are hereby repealed and abrogated. * * *
(Act Feb. 26, 1853, 10 Stat. at L. 164.)

JURORS' FEES.

For actual attendance at any court or courts, two dollars per day during such attendance.

For traveling from their residence to said court or courts, five cents per mile for going, and the same for returning.
(Act Feb. 26, 1853, 10 Stat. at L. 168.)

APPENDIX (A).

Witnesses' Fees.

For each day's attendance in court, or before any officer pursuant to law, one dollar and fifty cents, and five cents per mile for traveling from his place of residence to said place of trial or hearing, and five cents per mile for returning. When a witness is subpœnaed in more than one cause between the same parties in different suits at the same court, but one travel fee and one per diem compensation shall be allowed for attendance, to be taxed in the first case disposed of, and "per diem" only in the other causes, to be taxed from that time in each case, in the order in which they may be disposed of. (Act Feb. 26, 1853, 10 Stat. at L. 167.)

Printers' Fees.

For publishing any statute, notice or order required by law, or the lawful order of any court, department, bureau or other person, in any newspaper, forty cents per folio for the first insertion, and twenty cents per folio for each subsequent insertion. That the compensation herein provided shall include the furnishing lawful evidence, under oath, of publication, to be made and furnished by the printer or publisher making such publication.

The term folio, in this act, shall mean one hundred words, counting each figure as a word. When there are over fifty and under one hundred words, they shall be counted as one folio, but not when there are less, except when the whole statute notice or order contains less than fifty words. (Act Feb. 26, 1853, 10 Stat. at L. 168.)

Commissioners' Fees.

For administering an oath, ten cents; taking an acknowledgement, twenty-five cents.

For hearing and deciding on criminal charges, five dollars per day for the time necessarily employed.

APPENDIX (A). 163

For attending to a reference in a litigated matter in a civil cause at law, in equity, or in admiralty, in pursuance of an order of court, three dollars per day.

For taking and certifying depositions to file, twenty cents for each folio of one hundred words, and ten cents per folio for each copy of the same furnished to a party on request.

For issuing any warrant, or writ, or any other service, the same compensation as is allowed to clerks for like services.

For issuing any warrant under the tenth article of the treaty of the ninth of August, eighteen hundred and forty-two, between the United States and the Queen of the United Kingdom of Great Britain and Ireland, against any person charged with any of the crimes or offenses set forth in said article, two dollars; and the same sum for any warrant issued under the provisions of the convention for the surrender of criminals, between the United States and the King of the French, concluded at Washington on the ninth of November, eighteen hundred and forty-three; and for hearing and deciding upon the case of any person charged with any offense or crime, and arrested under the provisions of said treaty, or convention, five dollars per day for the time necessarily employed. (Act Feb. 26, 1853, 10 Stat. at L. 167.)

APPENDIX (B).

APPENDIX (B).

ORDER FOR PUBLICATION OF MARSHAL'S NOTICES.

UNITED STATES DISTRICT COURT, NORTHERN DISTRICT OF NEW YORK. MARCH TERM, 1869.

It is hereby ordered, that in all cases in which the Marshal is required to publish any notice of any process or proceeding, or any other notice, in any case pending on the common law or admiralty side of this court (other than in cases provided for by law or in the bankruptcy rules), the Marshal or his Deputy shall cause the same to be published as follows, viz.: In all cases in admiralty, except seizure cases, the notice of, or under the first process served or executed therein, shall be published in the county where such property was arrested under such process, and in the newspaper first named in the thirty-eighth general rule in bankruptcy heretofore adopted by this court as one of the newspapers in which notices in bankruptcy cases are, under said rule, to be published in said county; and in seizure cases in admiralty such notice shall be so published in the county where such seizure is illegal, in the information upon which such process was issued, to have been made, and in the newspaper therein first named in said bankruptcy rule as aforesaid; and all subsequent notices required to be published by the Marshal in either of such cases shall be published in the same paper. In all other than admiralty and bankruptcy cases, and in cases otherwise provided for by law, such notices of or under the first process or proceeding therein, and all subsequent notices in the same cause, shall be published in the county in which the property was arrested or seized as above first provided for in admiralty cases, except that such notices shall be published in the newspaper in such county secondly named in the said thirty-eighth bankruptcy rule, instead of the one firstly therein named. And in all cases where the first process is an execution or other process or order for the sale of real or personal property, or both, notices of sale under the same shall be published in the newspaper secondly named in said bankruptcy rules for publication of notices in the county in which such property may be seized under such execution, process or order.

In case any other newspaper has been, or shall hereafter be, substituted for one of the newspapers named in said bankruptcy rule, the publications in this rule referred to or provided for shall, in such case, be made in such substituted newspaper instead of the newspaper now mentioned in such bankruptcy rule.

But, notwithstanding the provisions hereinbefore contained, the judge of this court may in any case by writing, under his hand, direct any additional or different publication of any such notice; and whenever any such direction shall be given, such notice shall be published according to such direction. And in all cases not provided for by this order, or the general rules of this court, or by law, all such notices shall be published in such newspaper, and in such manner as said judge shall by writing direct; and in all cases in which such provision has not been made, the Marshal, before publishing such notice, shall apply for and obtain such direction.

All notices, unless otherwise provided by law, by the rules of court, or the special order of the court or the judge thereof, shall be published three times, and the first of such publications shall be made at as early a day as may be required by law or the rules and practice of the court.

APPENDIX (B). 169

And it is further ordered, that the Clerk certify a copy of the above, and of this order, and deliver the same to the Marshal of this District, and that in all seizure cases the Clerk shall indorse, on the first process issued therein, the name of the paper in which the notices in such cases are required to be published under the above order.

The thirty-eighth rule in bankruptcy, as it stands amended, and in so far as it is applicable to the foregoing order, requires that notices in cases of bankruptcy shall be published in the following named newspapers, viz. :

ALBANY COUNTY — In the Albany Evening Journal, and in the Argus.

ALLEGANY — In the Angelica Reporter, and in the Cuba Free Patriot.

BROOME — In the Binghamton Daily Republican, and in the Binghamton Democrat.

CAYUGA — In the Auburn Daily Advertiser, and in the Northern Christian Advocate.

CATTARAUGUS — In the Cattaraugus Republican, and in the Cattaraugus Union.

CHAUTAUQUA — In the Jamestown Journal, and in the Mayville Sentinel.

CHENANGO — In the Telegraph and Chronicle, at Norwich, and in the Chenango Union, at Norwich.

CHEMUNG — In the Elmira Daily Advertiser, and in the Elmira Daily Gazette.

CLINTON — In the Plattsburgh Sentinel, and in the Plattsburgh Republican.

CORTLAND — In the Cortland Weekly Journal, and in the Cortland County Democrat.

DELAWARE — In the Delaware Republican, and in the Delaware Gazette.

ERIE — In the Buffalo Commercial Advertiser, and in the Buffalo Daily Courier.

ESSEX — In the Essex County Republican, and in the Elizabethtown Post.

FRANKLIN — In the Malone Palladium, and in the Franklin Gazette.

FULTON OR HAMILTON — In the Johnstown Independent, and in the Fulton County Democrat.

GENESEE — In the Batavia Advocate, and in the Spirit of the Times, published at Batavia.

HERKIMER — In the Journal and Courier, and in the Herkimer County Democrat.

JEFFERSON — In the Northern New York Journal, and in the Watertown Re-Union.

LEWIS — In the Journal and Republican, published at Lowville, and in the Lewis County Democrat.

LIVINGSTON — In the Western New York Advertiser, published at Dansville, and in the Union and the Constitution, published at Mount Morris.

MADISON — In the Republican, published at Hamilton, and in the Madison Observer.

MONROE — In the Rochester Daily Union and Advertiser, and in the Rochester Daily Democrat.

MONTGOMERY — In the Montgomery County Republican, and in the Montgomery Democrat, published at Fonda.

NIAGARA — In the Lockport Union, and in the Lockport Journal.

ONTARIO — In the Ontario Repository and Messenger, at Canandaigua, and in the Geneva Courier.

ONIEDA — In the Utica Morning Herald, and in the Utica Daily Observer.

OSWEGO — In the Oswego Commercial Advertiser and Times, and in the Oswego Palladium.

ONONDAGA — In the Syracuse Daily Standard, and in the Syracuse Daily Courier and Union.

OTSEGO — In the Otsego Republican, and in the Freeman's Journal, published at Cooperstown.

ORLEANS — In the Orleans American, and in the Orleans Republican.

RENSSELAER — In the Troy Daily Times, and in the Troy Daily Press.

APPENDIX (B). 171

SCHOHARIE — In the Schoharie Republican, and in the Schoharie Union.

SCHENECTADY — In the Schenectady Daily Union, and in the Evening Star, published at Schenectady.

SARATOGA — In the Saratogian, and in the Saratoga Sentinel, published at Saratoga Springs.

ST. LAWRENCE — In the Courier and Freeman, published at Potsdam, and in the Ogdensburgh Advance.

SENECA — In the Seneca County Courier, and in the Seneca Observer.

STEUBEN — In the Canisteo Valley Times, and in the Steuben Farmers' Advocate.

SCHUYLER — In the Havana Journal, and in the Watkins Independent, or in the Schuyler County Democrat.

TIOGA — In the Owego Times, and in the Owego Gazette.

TOMPKINS — In the Ithaca Journal, and in the Ithaca Democrat.

WASHINGTON — In the Salem Press, and in the Sandy Hill Herald.

WARREN — In the Glens Falls Messenger, and in the Glens Falls Republican.

WAYNE — In the Lyons Weekly Republican, and in the Wayne Democratic Press.

WYOMING — In the New Yorker, published at Warsaw, and in the Democrat, published at the same place.

YATES — In the Penn Yan Express, and in the Penn Yan Democrat.

INDEX.

A

	PAGE.
Accounts, to be certified by district judge............................	52
may be appealed to secretary interior.....................	53
to be forwarded to first auditor when United States are liable for fees...	160
Acknowledgments, who have power to take.........................	24
Actions, of the different kinds of....................................	81
against property, when may be consolidated................	82
Admiralty, of actions in...	81
of warrant in..	22
custody fees in..	22
insurance on vessel in..................................	23
clerk district court may make rules in, when.............	25
when imprisonment for debt allowed in...................	55
Affidavits, who have power to take........................... 24, 25,	26
Appeal, lies from decision of accounting officer to secretary interior...	53
Appraisal, of goods taken on *fi. fa*................................	43
Appraisers, fees of...	43
Arrest, of... 28,	29
proceedings on, of judgment debtor in foreign district.........	36
Attachment, against witness..	31
when may issue against property of postmasters and post-office employees......................................	31
duty of marshal thereunder...........................	32
forms of returns to 91,	92
return to, against witness, form of.....................	136
Attorneys, fees of 52,	152

B

Bail, of...	33
where should reside	33
may surrender principal, mode of proceeding	33
in what cases admitted................................... 34,	35
when may be taken by State judge	34
new, when criminal may be required to give	35
how to procure discharge of, where principal committed in foreign district 36,	37

174　　　　　　　　　INDEX.

	PAGE.
Bail, delivery on, United States a party	22
who have power to take	24, 34
in civil actions	28
of marshal, liable for his acts in both districts after division of State	75
Bailiffs, to be appointed by marshal	157
Bailiff, may be deputized to serve process	79
Bankruptcy, commissioners may take proof of debts in	25
newspapers mentioned in 38th rule of	169
Bond of deputy marshal	19
Bond to marshal, form of, in civil cases	127

C

Ca. sa., service of 29
　　marshal cannot detain defendant for poundage, when 75
　　returns to, form of 143, 144
Capias, service of bailable 28
　　service of non-bailable....................................... 28
　　forms of returns to criminal........................... 124, 125
　　deputy marshal has no right to receive debt on 75
　　forms of returns to civil 126, 127, 129, 130
Capital cases, where to be tried.................................... 53
　　　　how many challenges allowed in 60
　　　　excessive challenges in, to be disallowed 60
　　　　limitations in 64
Certiorari, form of return to writ of 132
Challenges, how many allowed in capital cases 60
　　　　how many allowed in other cases 60
　　　　to be tried by the court 60, 61
　　　　excessive, in capital cases to be disallowed 60
　　　　how many allowed in summary trials 61
　　　　additional causes of, established 61
Chancellor of State court, may take depositions *de bene esse*........... 26
　　　　　　may take bail............................. 34
Circuit court, deputy marshal is an officer of 73
Citizenship, how to procure restoration to, of person convicted of crime 70
Civil suits, for acts done under authority of the President, etc., during
　　　　late rebellion, when to be commenced 65
Clerk, accounts of, to be certified by district judge.................. 52
　　in executive department detailed to investigate fraud, may administer oaths.. 69
Clerks, fees and emoluments of..................................... 158
　　to make return of emoluments every half year............... 158
　　fees of, to be allowed to, for each calendar year 159
Clerk of court may tax bills of costs................................. 160

INDEX. 175

	PAGE.
Clerk of district court, when may make rules in admiralty	25
Clerks of district and circuit courts authorized to administer oaths, take acknowledgemnts, affidavits, depositions	24, 25
of district and circuit courts, when may take special bail *de bene esse*	35
of district and circuit courts not to be allowed per diem at court sitting in bankruptcy, nor on rule days	159, 160
Common law, of actions at	81
Commissioners, fees of	52, 160
Commissioner authorized to administer oaths	69
how many United States witnesses allowed before	84
when may require recognizance from witness	85
Commissioners authorized to take bail, affidavits, depositions	24, 34
may take proof of debts in bankruptcy	25
authorized to arrest, imprison and bail offenders	30
authority to hold to security of the peace and good behavior	36
authorized to decide cases of extradition	49
may compel witnesses to depose to letters rogatory	88
Commissioners' courts, witness in, when to be paid	20
number witnesses for U. S. allowed in	20
duty of deputy marshal in	20
Consular officer authorized to administer oaths, take affidavits, depositions and perform notarial acts	26
Costs, clerk of court may tax bills of	160
bills of, to be sworn to	161
Court, prisoner to be brought to and from, without process	77
may sentence criminal to State prison or penitentiary, when	78
to appoint criers	157
Courts of United States have concurrent jurisdiction with State, in many cases	80
Courts of United States authorized to administer oaths	24
Court, Circuit, has no authority to take prisoner from State authority by *habeas corpus*, when	80
Courts, State, have no authority to take prisoner from United States custody	80
have concurrent jurisdiction with United States in many cases	80
Criers to be appointed by the court	157
compensation of	157
to be paid by marshal	157
to be paid but one per diem when in attendance on both courts	157
Crimes and offenses, who have jurisdiction of	30
Criminal may be arrested by bail; mode of proceeding	33
when may be required to give new bail	35

	PAGE.
Criminal sentenced for longer than one year may be imprisoned in State prison or penitentiary.	77
Criminals, United States, to be subject to same discipline as State prisoners.	77
to be under control of the officers of prison or penitentiary.	77
to have a deduction of one month per year, when and how	78
Criminal suits for acts done under authority of President, etc., during late rebellion, when to be commenced.	65
Criminal cases, judgment or sentence in, to be deemed judgment debt.	59
judgment or sentence in, may be collected on execution.	59

D

Decrees, in United States courts, when cease to be liens.	58
Deed of a vessel, form of.	112, 114, 116
Deed, when new marshal to execute deed to purchaser.	46
Depositions, who have power to take.	24, 25, 26
Deputy marshal, form of oath of.	17
oath of, before whom to be taken	18
of bond of	19
of bond of, form of.	121
books and papers of	19
duty of, at court	20, 21
duty of, on warrant in admiralty.	22
is an officer of United States.	71
may serve process	79
may return process, as deputy	71
has same powers as deputy sheriff	71
amenable to jurisdiction of district court.	71
amenable to jurisdiction of circuit court	73
to continue in office, on marshal's death	74
may execute process in his hands on marshal's death	48, 75
may complete sale, on death of marshal	48
may serve summons after new marshal appointed, when.	73
duty of, on completing sale.	83
may be attached for neglect to pay over money.	72
may sell on execution after return day	44
duty of, on arrest and commital of judgment debtor.	36
duty of, on completing panels of jurors.	63
duty of, where State court attempts to usurp jurisdiction of prisoner in his hands under extradition.	49

INDEX. 177

	PAGE.
Deputy marshal, duty of, as to appraisal of goods on *fi. fa.*	43
duty of, on distress warrants	38, 39, 40
duty of, on attachment against property of postmasters, etc.	32
has no right to receive debt on *capias*	75
See "Marshal."	
Deputization, form of special	136
Disclaimer, form of	125
Distress warrants, of	38
when and by whom issued	38
duty of deputy marshal on	38, 39, 40
when injunction may issue to stay, mode of proceeding	40, 41
form of solicitor's	146
District attorney, fees and emoluments of	152, 158
to make return of emoluments every half year	158
when to certify to materiality of United States witnesses	84
accounts of, to be certified by district judge	52
fees of, to be allowed to, for each calendar year	159
to be allowed but one per diem when district and circuit court sit at the same time	160
not to be allowed per diem at court sitting in bankruptcy, nor on rule days	159, 160
District court, deputy marshal is an officer of	71

E

Execution of, and proceedings thereon	43
when may run into any other State	45
when may run into any other district	45
marshal's sale on, when may be set aside	45
marshal may sell on, after return day	44
after removal, marshal may sell on	47, 48
deputy make complete sale on, on marshal's death	48
as to liability of marshal on	76
proceedings on, where marshal dies	46
is never completed until money is made and paid over	47
when imprisonment for debt is allowed on	55
when prisoner may be discharged from imprisonment on	55
when interest may be levied on, in civil cases	54
forms of returns to	138, 139, 140
Exemption governed by State laws	44
Equity, of service of writ of subpœna in	80
Extension of time of finding indictments in late rebel States	65

178 INDEX.

	PAGE.
Extradition, who authorized to decide cases of	49
prisoner under, when to be removed	50
prisoner under, when may be discharged	50
expenses of, by whom defrayed	50
certain persons invested with powers of marshal in cases of	51

F

Fee, marshal and clerk not to charge fee for the bringing of prisoner into court	77
Fees, custody, in admiralty	22
who entitled to, on arrest of fugitive	30
of marshal on attachment of property of postmasters, etc.	33
of marshal on committing judgment-debtor from foreign district,	37
of appraisers	43
of attorneys, solicitors and proctors	52, 151
of district attorneys	52, 152
of clerks	52, 153
of marshals	52, 154
and emoluments of district attorneys, clerks and marshals	158
district attorneys, clerks and marshals to make return of, every half year	158
allowance of, to district attorneys, clerks and marshals to be for each calendar year	159
bills of, to be taxed by judge or clerk	160
where United States are liable, to be paid on forwarding accounts to first auditor	160
penalty for demanding excessive	161
bills of, to be sworn to	161
penalty for making false affidavit to bill of	161
of jurors	52, 161
of witnesses	52, 162
of printers	52, 82, 162
of commissioners	52, 162
Foreman of grand jury to be appointed by court	60
of grand jury authorized to administer oaths	60
Forfeiture cases, limitation in	64
Forgery of seal or signature of secretary of legation or consular officer, where to be punished	27
Form of returns to attachment	92
of notices of seizure	93, 105
of return to warrant of monition	94
of return to warrant of sale	95, 96
of notice of sale	96

INDEX.   179

	PAGE.
Form of notice of postponement of sale	97
of bill and affidavit of storekeeper	97
of marshal's bill in information suit	98
of returns to warrant of arrest and monition	103, 104
of return to monition	106
of notice on monition	106
of return to *venditioni exponas*	107
of notice of sale	108
of bill and affidavit of ship keeper	108
of returns to warrant in personam	109, 110
of marshal's bill in admiralty	111
of deed of vessel	112, 114, 116
of deputy marshal's bond	121
of returns to criminal *capias*	124, 125
of disclaimer	125
of returns to civil *capias*	126, 127, 129, 130
of bond to marshal, civil cases	127
of marshal's bill in civil cases	130
of return to summons	131
of return to writ of subpœna in equity	132
of return to writ of certiorari	132
of return to venire	133
of certificate to jury panels	133
of notice to jurors	134
of return to subpœna	134
of subpœna ticket, United States cases	134
of subpœna tickets, private suits	135
of notice to be indorsed on subpœna ticket, United States cases,	135
of receipt for prisoner	136
of attachment against witness	136
of special deputization	136
of oath to jurors on writ of inquiry	137
of oath to witnesses on writ of inquiry	137
of writ of inquiry	137
of inquisition	138
of returns to execution	138, 139, 140
of indorsement of levy	140
of receipt for property levied on	141
of notice of sale of personal property	142
of notice of sale of real estate	143
of returns of *ca. sa.*, form of	143, 144
of warrant of district judge for removal of prisoner to foreign district	144
of marshal's return to same	146
of solicitor's distress warrant	146

                                                                    PAGE.
Frauds, limitation of actions for certain........................ 67
Fugitive, proceedings to arrest 29

G

Grand jury, of how many persons to consist 59
    of, generally 60
    when talesmen may be summoned for 60
    court to appoint foreman of.............................. 60
    foreman of, authorized to administer oath 60

H

Habeas corpus, marshal bound to make return to, from State court.... 76
    United States court cannot take prisoner from State
        custody by, when 80

I

Indictments, of... 53
    in capital cases... 53
    may be found in district or circuit court................ 53
    how many jurors necessary to find........................ 60
    may be tried in district or circuit court................ 53
    in capital cases to be tried in circuit court 53
    in capital cases, when to be found....................... 64
    in cases not capital, when to be found................... 64
    in late rebel States, when to be found 65
    when several charges to be joined in one................. 54
Injunction, when may issue to stay distress warrant.............. 41
Insurance, on vessel 23
Interest, when may be levied in civil cases...................... 54
Imprisonment for debt, of.. 55
            when allowed 55
            where abolished.................................. 55
            proceedings to discharge from 56
Inquisition, form of... 138

J

Jails, of 56
    when marshal may hire place for.......................... 57
    expenses for, when allowed to marshal.................... 57
    marshal has no control over prisoner committed to State.. 77
Jail, State, marshal in, no longer in custody of prisoner committed to. 72
    marshal not liable for escape of debtor from............. 72
    keeper of, is not deputy of the marshal 72

INDEX. 181

	PAGE.
Judge of United States, may order discharge of prisoner under extradition, when	50
Judge of United States court, may issue warrant against witness, when	85
when may require recognizance from witness	85, 86
may take bail	34
Judges of the district courts, authorized to decide cases of	49
Judges of the United States supreme and district courts, authorized to hold to security of the peace and good behavior	35
Judges and justices of State courts, authorized to hold to security of the peace and good behavior	35
Judge of State court, may take bail, and when	34
may order discharge of prisoner under extradition, when	50
authorized to decide cases of extradition	49
Judge of county court, may take depositions *de bene esse*	26
of court of common pleas, may take depositions *de bene esse*	26
Judge, chief judge of court of common pleas, may take bail	34
Judgments, in United States courts, when cease to be liens	58
in criminal cases, how may be collected	59
interest, when may be levied on, in civil cases	54
may be collected from interest of co-partner in the goods	59
Judgment-debtor, proceedings on committal in foreign district	36
how long to be held in custody in foreign district	37
Jurors, fees of	52, 161
from what part of district to be drawn	62
writs of *venire facias* for, to issue from clerk's office	62
writs of *venire facias* for, by whom served	62, 63
qualifications of, in United States courts	62
how designated	62, 63
courts have power to make rules in reference to designation and impaneling of	62
how many challenges to, allowed in summary trials	61
additional causes of challenge to, established	61
challenges to, to be tried by the court	60
challenges to, how many allowed in capital cases	60
excessive, in capital cases, to be disallowed	60
to be paid by marshal	160
duty of deputy marshal on completing panels of	63
how summoned in northern district of New York	63
Jury, grand, of how many persons to consist	59
when talesmen may be summoned for	60
court to appoint foreman of	60
foreman of, authorized to administer oaths	60
of grand, generally	60

182　INDEX.

	PAGE.
Jury panels, form of certificate to	133
Jurisdiction of United States and State courts	80
Justice of United States court, when may require recognizance of witness	85
Justice or judge of United States authorized to arrest, imprison and bail offenders	30
Justice or judge of United States court may take depositions *de bene esse*	26
Justice or judge of State court may take depositions *de bene esse*	26
Justices of the supreme court authorized to decide cases of extradition,	49
Justice of the peace authorized to arrest, imprison and bail offenders..	30
Juvenile offenders to be confined in house of refuge	78

L

Letters rogatory, commissioners may compel witness to depose to	88
Levy may be made on interest of copartner in the goods	59
indorsement of, form of	140
Liability, as to, of marshal on execution	76
Lien, when to run, in case of officers failing to pay over money	39
when sheriff has prior	59
when judgments and decrees in United States courts cease to be liens	58
Limitation, in capital cases	64
in capital cases, when to take effect	64
in cases not capital	64
in penalty and forfeiture cases	65
of suits on marshal's bonds	66
of suits against sureties of postmasters, not considered as running in any State in rebellion	66
of suits against sureties of postmasters	67
of actions for certain frauds	67
of suits for acts done under authority of the President, etc., during the late rebellion	65
of actions during the late rebellion, explained and defined.	66

M

Marshal, may appoint special deputy	79
to appoint bailiffs	157
to be allowed fees for summoning jurors, United States witnesses, defendant's witnesses, and for maintenance of prisoners	155
fees of	52, 154
to be allowed expenses of holding courts	158
to be allowed expenses of rent, furniture, etc., how much	158

INDEX. 183

	PAGE.
Marshal, fees and emoluments of	158
to make return of emoluments every half year	158
to be allowed expenses for endeavoring to arrest criminal	157
fees of, to be allowed to, for each calendar year	159
not to charge fee for bringing prisoner to and from court	77
not to be allowed per diem at court sitting in bankruptcy, nor on rule days	159, 160
may accept actual expenses in lieu of fees	155
accounts of, to be certified by district judge	52
to pay jurors and witnesses	160
to pay defendant's witnesses, when	84
where, or deputy is a party, process to be directed to disinterested person	80
as to liability of, on execution	76
may levy on interest of copartner in the goods	59
sheriff has prior lien over, when	59
cannot detain defendant on *ca. sa.* for poundage, when	75
has power to summon *posse comitatus*	72
to be allowed expense for transportation of convicts, etc.	58
to return writ for removal of prisoner, to the clerk of the district to which removal is made.	79
to transport juvenile offenders to house of refuge	78
is no longer in custody of prisoner committed to State jail	72
has no control over prisoner committed to State jail	77
not liable for escape of debtor from State jail	72
keeper of the State jail is not deputy of the	72
is responsible only for his own and deputies' acts	72
responsible for delivery of prisoner to his successor	75
penalty on, for allowing prisoner to escape	73
to deliver copy of process on committing prisoner	78, 79
to deliver copy of process on removing prisoner	79
bound not to obey State process	76
when may hire jails	57
when to be allowed expenses for jails	57
to make return to *habeas corpus* from State court	76
have same powers as sheriffs	71
is not removed until he receives notice	74
certain persons invested with powers of, in cases of extradition	51
to give notice of seizure	81
to give notice of sale	82
marshal's duty on employing storekeeper	82
publication of notices of, in northern district New York	83, 167
to serve writs of *venire facias*	63
limitation of suits on bond of	66
has no authority to warrant	74

184 INDEX.

	PAGE.
Marshal to execute warrant against witness	86
continued in office as marshal of both districts after division of State	75
in case of death of, deputies to continue in office	75
executor or administrator of, to have remedy against deputy for malfeasance (see "Deputy Marshal")	74
Marshal's bill, form of, in civil cases	130
form of, in admiralty	111
form of, in information suit	98
Magistrate of any State authorized to arrest, imprison and bail offenders	30
Mayor of a city may take depositions *de bene esse*	26
may take bail	34
Monition, form of return to	106

N

Name, law knows of but one christian	68
affix "Jr.," not essential to	68
Newspapers, mentioned in 38th bankruptcy rule	169
Notaries public, authorized to take depositions	24
authorized to administer oaths	68
seal and signature of, not sufficient evidence in cases of perjury	68
Notice, of sale by marshal	82
of sale, forms of	96, 108
of sale, how many days to be published	82
of sale of personal property, form of	142
of sale of real estate, form of	143
of postponement of sale, form of	97
of seizure by marshal, form of	82
of seizure, forms of	93, 105
to jurors, form of	134
of sale on *venditioni exponas*	23
marshal is not removed until he receives	74
on monition, form of	106
to be indorsed on subpœna ticket, United States cases, form of	135
Notices, of, publication of marshal's, in northern district, New York	83, 161

O

Oath, of deputy marshal, form of	17
of deputy marshal, before whom taken	18
Oaths, who have power to administer	24, 25, 26
may be taken before notary public	68
may be taken before commissioner	69

INDEX. 185

	PAGE.
Oaths may be taken before any department clerk or officer detailed to investigate frauds	69
foreman of grand jury authorized to administer	60
Office, deputy marshal to continue in, on death of marshal	74
Officer, of United States, when not to receive pay as witness	84
of United States courts, when not entitled to witness fees	85
Officers of United States, when clerks and other, not entitled to fees as witness	87
Officers of courts, of	81

P

Panels, duty of deputy marshal on completing	63
Pardons, the President alone has power to grant	69
mode of proceeding to obtain	69
may be granted by President as to either part of sentence	70
Penalty cases, limitation in	64
Penalty for allowing prisoner to escape	73
for attempting rescue of prisoner received from foreign government	51
for making false affidavit to bill of costs	159
for demanding excessive fees	159
Perjury before secretary of legation or consular officer, where to be punished	27
seal and signature of notary not sufficient evidence in cases of	68
Postmasters, limitations of suits against sureties of, not considered as running in any State in rebellion	66
limitation of suits against sureties	67
Poundage, marshal cannot detain defendant for, on *ca. sa.*, when	75
Power, marshal has, to summon *posse comitatus*	72
Powers of marshals and deputies same as sheriffs and deputies	72
of President in matters of extradition	50
Practice, of	44
President, powers of, in matters of extradition	50
alone has power to grant pardons	69
may grant pardons as either part of sentence	70
Printers, fees of	52, 160
Printer's fees, publishing notice of seizure	82
publishing notice of sale	82
Prison, officers of State, and penitentiaries to have exclusive jurisdiction over United States prisoners	77
Prisoner, removal of, from foreign district	29, 30
to be brought to and from court without process	77
only one writ necessary for arrest and committal of	79
only one writ necessary for removal of, from one district to another	79

INDEX.

	PAGE.
Prisoner, when committed to jail marshal to deliver a copy of the writ,	78
marshal no longer in custody of, when committed to State jail	72, 77
under extradition, when to be removed	50
under extradition, when may be discharged	50
penalty on marshal for allowing escape of	73
received from foreign government, penalty for attempting rescue of	51
marshal bound to make return to *habeas corpus* for	76
Prisoners, marshal responsible for delivery of, to his successor	75
sentenced in United States courts, where to be imprisoned	58
sentenced in United States courts, where may be imprisoned,	58
United States, to be subject to same discipline as those of State and to be under control of officers of the prisons	77
Process, how and where served	79
execution and return of	19
not to be altered	21
of final, and proceedings thereon	43
deputy marshal bound to execute, as directed	75
may be returned by deputy marshal as deputy	71
deputy may execute, in his hands on marshal's death	48, 75
marshal may execute, in his hands on removal	48
marshal to deliver copy of, on committing prisoner	78
to be returned by marshal with his return indorsed	78
division of, as to liability of marshal	76
only one necessary for removal of prisoner from one district to another	79
when marshal or deputy is a party, to be directed to disinterested person	80
where marshal to return, for removal of prisoner from one district to another	79
only one necessary for arrest and committal of prisoner	79
marshal is bound not to obey State	76
Publication of marshal's notices in northern district New York	165

R

Receipt for prisoner, form of	136
for property levied on, form of	141
Registers in bankruptcy authorized to administer oaths	25
Return, marshal to make, to process	78
of, to *venditioni exponas*	23
Rule, newspapers mentioned in the 38th bankruptcy rule	167

S

Sale, marshal's duty on	82
duty of deputy marshal on completing	83
notice of, how many days to be published	82
when new marshal to perfect	46
marshal may make, after his removal	47, 48

INDEX. 187

	PAGE.
Sale, deputy may complete, on death of marshal	48
Seamen, what compensation allowed to, as witnesses	87
when to be allowed sustenance and transportation as witness,	88
Security of the peace, who may hold to	35
Secretary of interior may designate prisons for confinement of United States convicts	53
to approve of deduction from sentence of United States criminals	78
to designate house of refuge for confinement of juvenile offenders	78
Secretary of legation, authorized to administer oaths, take affidavits, depositions and perform notarial acts	26
Seizure, of	80
marshal's duty on making	81
Sentence, of criminal for more than one year, may be to State prison or penitentiary	77
expenses of sentence to be paid by United States	78
United States criminals to have deduction of one month per year from, when and how	78
Sentence fine, how may be collected	59
Sheriff, has prior lien, when	59
Ship-keeper, form of bill and affidavit of	108
Solicitor of the treasury, when to issue distress warrants	38
in discretion of, to issue distress warrants	42
form of distress warrant of	146
Special bail, when clerks of district and circuit courts may take	35
State court, has no jurisdiction over prisoner in custody of marshal under extradition	49
Store-keeper, marshal's duty on employing	82
amount to be paid	82
form of bill and affidavit of	97
Subpœnas, by whom issued	21
where to run	83
in civil cases, where to run	83
as many names of witnesses to be inserted in, as possible	153
for defendant's witnesses, when may be ordered at United States expense	83
form of return to	134
Subpœna in equity, form of return to writ of	132
Subpœna ticket, United States cases, form of	134
private suits, form of	135
Summons, when deputy marshal may serve summons after new marshal appointed	73
form of return to	13

T

Talesmen, when may be summoned for grand jury	60
Terms, of the definition of certain	81

INDEX.

V

	PAGE.
Venditioni exponas, notice of sale under	23
of return to	23
of return to, form of	107
Venire, form of return to	133
Venire facias, writs of, to issue from clerk's office	62
to be served by marshal or his deputy	62
when to be served by some other person	63

W

Warrant, when and by whom warrant may issue against 86
    marshal has no authority to 74
    there is no, on marshal's sale 45
    in admiralty, duty of deputy marshal on 22
    of monition, form of return to 04
    of sale, forms of returns to 95, 96
    of district judge to remove prisoner to foreign district, form of, 144
    of district judge to remove prisoner to foreign district, form
        of return thereto 146
    of arrest and monition, forms of return to 103, 104
    in personam, forms of returns to 109, 110
Witness, for United States to be subpœnaed generally 86
    for United States to appear before either jury as required ... 86
    detained witness, to what compensation entitled 87
    not to be excluded on account of color 84
    fees of 52, 160
    to be paid by marshal 158
    as many names to be inserted in subpœna as possible 153
    United States, how many allowed before commissioner 84
    for United States in commissioner's court, when to be paid .. 20
    for United States in commissioner's court, number allowed .. 20
    for United States to be subpœnaed but once 21
    when and by whom may be required to give recognizance, 85, 86
    attachment against 31
    for defendant detained, entitled to same fees as United States
        witnesses 85
    for defendant, when may be subpœnaed at United States
        expense 83
    when officer of United States courts not entitled to fees as, 84, 85
    clerks and other United States officers, when not entitled to
        fees as 87
    seamen, what compensation allowed to as 87
    seamen, when to be allowed sustenance and transportation as, 88
Writ of inquiry, form of oath to jurors on 137
    form of oath to witnesses on 137
    form of return to 137
Writ of subpœna, of service of, in equity 80

www.ingramcontent.com/pod-product-compliance
Lightning Source LLC
Chambersburg PA
CBHW031438160426
43195CB00010BB/775